THE VICTORIAN GARDEN

Caroline Ikin

SHIRE PUBLICATIONS

Published in Great Britain in 2012 by Shire Publications Ltd, Midland House, West Way, Botley, Oxford OX2 0PH, United Kingdom.

44-02 23rd Street, Suite 219, Long Island City, NY 11101, USA.

E-mail: shire@shirebooks.co.uk   www.shirebooks.co.uk

A CIP catalogue record for this book is available from the British Library.

Shire Library no. 691.   ISBN-13: 978 0 74781 152 7

Caroline Ikin has asserted her right under the Copyright, Designs and Patents Act, 1988, to be identified as the author of this book.

Designed by Tony Truscott Designs, Sussex, UK and typeset in Perpetua and Gill Sans.

Printed in China through Worldprint Ltd.

12 13 14 15 16   10 9 8 7 6 5 4 3 2 1

COVER IMAGE
The garden at Trentham in Staffordshire, designed by Charles Barry in 1840, was a celebrated example of the Victorian Italianate style, combining architectural features with massed bedding.

TITLE PAGE IMAGE
Colourful bedding plants were popularised in the Victorian era, with many new species and cultivars introduced.

CONTENTS PAGE IMAGE
A group of working gardeners photographed among the flowers in a walled garden.

ACKNOWLEDGEMENTS
My thanks to Philip Norman at the Garden Museum for all his help with the illustrations, to Ed Ikin for botanical clarification, and to Linda Cousins for her invaluable contributions.

Shire Publications is supporting the Woodland Trust, the UK's leading woodland conservation charity, by funding the dedication of trees.

CONTENTS

PART ONE

A CHANGING SOCIETY

AFTER VICTORY AT THE Battle of Waterloo, the people of Britain had enjoyed many years of peace and prosperity. Inflation was low, as was taxation, and the boom in manufacturing led to expanding markets and rising wages. During the sixty-four years of her reign (1837–1901), Queen Victoria oversaw developments which were to elevate Britain to a position of economic supremacy, but which also fostered consequences of social hardship, poverty and deprivation.

People were attracted to the newly expanding towns and cities where they could find work in factories and industry: when land was taken away from the poor by the Enclosure Act of 1845, there was little work in the depressed agricultural communities. Urban areas soon became overcrowded, filthy, and rife with disease and pollution. Those with the means to do so escaped the squalor and ugliness of urban life, commuting via the newly extended rail network to homes and gardens in the fresh air and prosperity of the suburbs. This newly emerging stratum of society included those who made their money through managing factories, and in the associated trades of banking and insurance, and they formed the new middle class. The upper classes were profiting from the mineral wealth mined from their lands, as well as from investments in railways and property development. The creation of a garden was an ideal way for the bourgeois to announce their arrival and for the aristocracy to emphasise their ancestral ownership.

At the height of the social structure were the Victorian super-rich. Many estate owners had increased their fortunes by selling the coal extracted from their land, which was now a commodity in industrial Britain, or through shrewd investments in transport and manufacturing. Others had profited through slavery and the exploitation of foreign lands, or generated money in banking. Great fortunes led to extravagance and experimentation in gardens, where wealth was displayed through bedding schemes, parterre design, elaborate terracing, vast glasshouses and the cultivation of exotic species.

The sixth Duke of Devonshire had added to his considerable fortune by the mining of coal on his estates. The bachelor duke led an extravagant

Opposite:
The participation of children in healthy and educational garden tasks is shown in a watercolour by Lucien Besche of c. 1890, as well as displaying the Victorian fondness for potted plants.

Next spread:
Hamstead Old Rectory, shown in a painting of 1863, illustrates a typical middle-class garden with a well-tended lawn and irregular flower beds.

5

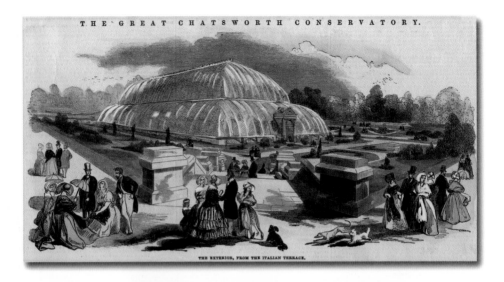

THE GREAT CHATSWORTH CONSERVATORY.

THE EXTERIOR, FROM THE ITALIAN TERRACE.

The Great Conservatory, designed by Paxton and constructed in 1840, was the most impressive feature in the garden at Chatsworth, and the largest glasshouse in the world.

The water tree at Chatsworth exemplifies Paxton's mastery over nature in a garden designed to impress.

lifestyle, and laid out an extravagant garden at Chatsworth in Derbyshire, the duke supplying the money and his head gardener Joseph Paxton contributing the genius. Together they created impressive and celebrated garden features including the Emperor Fountain, with a jet rising to a height of over eighty metres, a vast area of rockwork incorporating the enormous Wellington Rock, a metal tree which squirted water at unsuspecting passers-by, and a rock which revolved with a gentle push to reveal a concealed path beyond. The most acclaimed feature of the garden was the Great Conservatory, completed in 1840. At 84 metres long, 37 metres wide and 19 metres high, it was the largest glasshouse in the world, and was the model for the Crystal Palace – housing the Great Exhibition of 1851 – which brought Paxton international success and a knighthood.

The garden created at Trentham in Staffordshire was another ostentatious display of old money supplemented by a fortune made through the Industrial Revolution. The Duke of Sutherland had prospered from investment in canals to such an extent that he could afford to engage the architect Charles Barry to remodel his house and, from 1840, to create a garden of national renown. Trentham was laid out in the Italianate style, with sweeping terraces lined with balustrades and statues leading from the house to the lake, where a gondolier was employed to embellish the view. On the terraces were elaborate parterres filled with impressive displays of bedding plants. The sheer numbers of plants demanded by these designs, and the labour required to raise, plant and maintain the parterres, were a colourful testament to the wealth and status of the owner.

The Rothschilds had made their money in banking and were considered to have amassed the largest private fortune in the world. The family lavished their riches on the creation of several houses and gardens, the ostentatious

1. *Coleus Verschaffeltii Improved.*
2. *Leucophyton Brownii.*
3. *Alternanthera paronychioides major.*
4. *Pyrethrum Golden Feather.*
5. *Echeveria secunda glauca.*
6. *Alternanthera amœna.*
7. *Mesembryanthemum cordifolium variegatum.*

1. *Echeveria glauco-metallica.*
2. *Pyrethrum Golden Feather.*
3. *Alternanthera amœna.*
4. *Antennaria tomentosa.*
5. *Sempervivum tabulæforme.*
6. *Echeveria secunda glauca.*

A design for carpet bedding from Robert Thompson's *Gardener's Assistant* of 1888 illustrates the complexity of Victorian bedding schemes and the colourful and impressive effects created by gardeners.

Baron Ferdinand de Rothschild commissioned Waddesdon Manor in 1874 to assert his wealth and accomplishment through architecture and garden design, displayed here in the elaborate fountain and ostentatious bedding.

With the new technology available, wealthy Victorians were able to create splendid displays of exotic plants to fill their impressive glasshouses, as shown in this illustration from 1880.

architecture complemented by extravagant bedding schemes. Many of these estates were established in Buckinghamshire, including Waddesdon Manor, Mentmore Towers and Halton House where, through architecture and garden design, the émigré family became firmly entrenched in British culture.

No problem was insurmountable to the Victorian super-rich: their wealth, combined with the inventive spirit of the age, enabled them to create impressive and astonishing features in their gardens. Vast glasshouses filled with displays of exotic plants were heated by boilers fed on coal delivered on trains running through underground tunnels, to avoid the intrusion of industry on the artful elegance of the garden.

New methods of transplanting mature trees were used to create an instant impression of mature, ancestral grounds.

Queen Victoria herself was interested in plants. She admired the natural landscape and had a fondness for wild flowers, but also cast a curious eye over the new species being introduced to Britain from abroad. In 1843 she visited Chatsworth where she watched as Joseph Paxton's young daughter stood on the huge leaf of the water lily *Victoria regia* (now known as *Victoria amazonica*), named in honour of the monarch. Prince Albert was a champion of the arts, including the art of gardening, and at Osborne on the Isle of Wight he created an Italianate garden to complement the house he had designed as a summer retreat for the royal family.

M'Nab's Transplanter.

A technique for transplanting large trees was developed in the 1830s, enabling instant mature gardens to be created by those keen to make an impression.

Queen Victoria encouraged her own children to be involved in the garden at Osborne on the Isle of Wight, where each child was supplied with garden tools and a monogrammed wheelbarrow.

An illustration from John Mollison's *Practical Window Gardener* of 1887 demonstrates how colour and variety could be brought to even the smallest urban garden.

An illustration from *The Amateur Flower Garden* by Shirley Hibberd, published in 1878, shows the level of control and artifice present in the Victorian garden, with architectural beds and flowers arranged in ribbon borders.

The middle classes wanted to establish themselves in society, using the style and scale of their houses and gardens to display taste and gentility. Many smaller country houses were built to the designs of the fashionable architects of the day to display an outward appearance of wealth. Garden style played a large part in this emulation of gentility, where acceptance in society might hinge on the colour and design of a bedding scheme. In the new suburbs, gardening was seen both as a suitable pastime for the middle classes and as a demonstration of taste and respectability.

The progress in industry and science which had provided the income to create gardens was also a catalyst for change in the possibilities and opportunities in gardening. New materials were developed for building roads, bridges, factories and houses, and these were also put to use in gardens. The introduction of asphalt in the late 1830s provided an ideal surface for garden paths, and concrete, developed in the 1840s, was the basis of the material used to create artificial rock gardens by James Pulham & Son. The tax on bricks was repealed in 1850, reducing the cost of garden walls and buildings, and developments in the manufacture of terracotta produced an affordable range of garden ornaments.

The abolition of the tax on glass in 1845, coupled with the invention of sheet glass in 1847, made possible the development of affordable glasshouses. The wrought-iron glazing bar was patented by the eminent garden writer John Loudon in 1816, but timber was the preferred material in glasshouse construction until the invention of an improved glass putty containing linseed oil, which countered the effects of expansion and contraction in metal glazing bars and safely held the glass in place. With the invention of cast iron, prefabricated glasshouse sections could be made and marketed by catalogue to

A page from the Austin & Seeley catalogue of 1844 illustrates the range of mass-produced terracotta garden ornaments available at reasonable cost to the Victorian homeowner.

gardeners of limited means, popularising the use of bedding and exotics in suburban gardens. The heating of larger glasshouses and conservatories was also improved in line with technological developments, from the early use of hot air flues, to a system of hot water pipes fed by coal boilers, which was eventually superseded by more efficient gas boilers.

Gardeners benefited enormously from the railway expansion of the 1840s

An advertisement, published in *Gardening Illustrated* in 1879, shows just one of many designs for glasshouses available at moderate cost to the Victorian gardener, facilitating the cultivation of tender and exotic plants.

The variety and colour of bedding plants available is illustrated in Carters' seed catalogue of 1898.

and 1850s. Plants could be ordered from a catalogue and delivered direct from the nursery in prime condition. Nurseries no longer needed to be based in towns and cities, and could instead relocate to areas with better growing conditions which were well served by the rail network. Companies such as the illustrious Veitch Nurseries operated from premises in Exeter and Surrey, while maintaining their London showroom for entertaining clients and displaying newly introduced plants. The nurseries and seed houses were also now able to engage representatives to travel the country promoting their goods and selling seeds and plants.

The railways also facilitated the visiting of gardens, many of which were opened to the public and popularised by the gardening press, and visits could

The advent of the railways facilitated the efficient delivery of plants and seeds ordered from nursery catalogues, giving choice and variety to gardeners all over Britain.

The introduction of the penny post enabled seed companies to offer free delivery of small packages, as illustrated in this advertisement from an 1880 edition of *Gardening Illustrated*.

Victorian children were encouraged to help in the garden, where they could benefit from fresh air and exercise, while learning important lessons about nature and the rewards of hard work.

be made to horticultural shows, whether to take part or to gain inspiration. The rich made use of the railways to ensure that their London tables were served with a steady supply of produce arriving in pristine condition from the kitchen gardens of their country estates.

In addition to the status they afforded, the pleasure they provided and the progress they represented, there was also another force at work in the promotion of gardens: the moral reformers championed the garden as a place of spiritual redemption and a release from the hardship of working life and a distraction from the temptations of vice. Gardening was seen as a wholesome occupation for mind and body, and as a healthy and educational pastime for women and children.

In the smoky, overcrowded cities gardens gave respite and clean air, and in the 1840s public parks began to appear in urban areas all over the country. These designed landscapes gave people the opportunity to exercise their bodies and rest their minds amid trees and flowers and to engage in boating on the lake, games on the playing fields, or tea in the refreshment rooms. Prior to the introduction of public parks, there was very little accessible green space in towns and cities, as pleasure gardens charged admission and the gardens of city squares were the privilege of residents only. The provision of parks was seen by the social reformers as vital to the moral and spiritual wellbeing of the nation, and gardens were regarded by the Victorians as an important dimension of social welfare.

Visits to flower shows were a popular pastime, where floral displays were often accompanied by other entertainments, as shown in this poster from 1840.

No. 11100.—Rotary Garden Fumigator. By turning the handle the blower sends a continuous current of sulphur, contained in cup, into plants, killing insects, &c. Japanned bronze green.

No. 11103.—Watering Pot, with long spout, and brass rose to unscrew, japanned green or red, strongly made.

No. 11102.—Garden Watering Pot, strong, japanned red or green.

No. 11101.—Fumigating Dre sulphur contained handle.

No. 11104.—Strawberry Watering Pot strong, japanned red or green, wi hood.

No. 11105.—The Coventry Lawn Mower, specially adapted for cutting long or short grass, will turn in its own width, and very easy to work.

No. 11106. — Improved Geared Lawn Mower, with patent silent ratchet. This machine is suitable for cutting grass which is very rough and coarse. The wheels are contained in a box, which deadens the noise usually accompanying geared machines.

No. 11108.—Improved Garden Roller, with shafts for horse, pony, or donkey. Double Cylinder. Being made in two parts, these rollers are free to turn on their own axis, and obviates the dragging motion produced on gravel or grass by the single cylinder roller.

No. 11109.—Double Cylinder Garden Roller, wit balance handles.

No. 11107.—Single Cylinder Garden Roller, with balance handles.

No. 11110.—Swing Water Barrow with Improved Hand Pump, complete, with lever, spreader, and 18 inches of delivery hose, capable of throwing a jet of water 40 feet.

No. 11111.—Improved Galvanized Wrought-iron Tank on Wheels, with shafts for pony or horse, with pump and 10 feet suction hose, galvanized, wired inside.

S. & F.
London.

TRADE MARK

No. 11112.—Galvanized Tank on Wheels, with shafts for a pony or horse, suitable for conveying water or liquid manure to gardens, &c. This barrow is remarkably compact, will turn in its own length, and will pass through any garden door of ordinary width.

No. 11113.—Galvan Wrought-iron Tank, on wheels, with valve and spr

HORTICULTURAL ADVANCEMENTS

THE PIONEERING ENERGY OF Victorian invention and enquiry led to huge advancements in the technical achievements of horticulture. Scientific knowledge added to the experience and observations of generations of gardeners, and an understanding of the physiology of plants and the composition of soil resulted in modern methods of cultivation. Scientific advances were also beginning to throw into question established religious belief: the discovery of fossils was prompting geologists to cast doubt on the theory of creation, and Charles Darwin added fuel to the debate in his ground-breaking work *On the Origin of Species*, published in 1859. Discoveries in animal and plant evolution led to experiments in selection and hybridisation, and non-native seeds brought to Britain by plant hunters were successfully raised and introduced.

Although experiments in the eighteenth century had proved that plants absorb carbon dioxide from the air and release oxygen, further advances were hampered by a lack of fundamental understanding and scientific rigour, and by detractors with creationist beliefs. Until the 1840s it was generally accepted that plants took in nutrients through the air and disposed of waste matter through their roots. Further experimentation finally delivered more accurate theories of plant nutrition, and in 1860 the process of photosynthesis was understood.

Most professional gardeners relied on their own experience, using methods which produced results, regardless of whether they understood the reasons behind their success. The increasing popular interest in gardening, together with the practical need to feed a growing population, fuelled horticultural research. In 1843, John Bennet Lawes established a series of experiments in soil science on his estate at Rothamsted which led to the development of effective fertilisers and had a significant impact on crop production. Aided by the expertise of chemist Joseph Gilbert, Lawes demonstrated that plants absorb nitrogen from the soil and not from the air, and recognised the importance of potash and phosphates in the soil. With a greater understanding of the importance of soil fertility, a popular demand for fertiliser was created and the

Opposite:
As the popularity of gardening increased, a new market for tools and gadgets developed, providing an outlet for Victorian inventors. A page from the Silber & Flemming catalogue of 1883 illustrates the variety of equipment available to gardeners.

commercial production of fertilisers began. In 1842, Lawes patented an artificial fertiliser made from bonemeal, and he marketed other products containing mineral phosphates. Then, in 1845, Lawes commenced commercial extraction of fossilised animal droppings known as coprolites, which had been discovered in East Anglia and could be used to enrich soil. The waste product from the steel manufacturing process – known as slag – was also found to contain minerals which could be used as fertiliser, and was marketed in the 1880s.

The benefits of enriching the soil with animal manure, lime and chalk had been recognised for generations. Manure was in plentiful supply in Victorian times, particularly from horses, but pig and cow dung was also used, as was the euphemistically named 'nightsoil'. Perhaps the most significant animal fertiliser introduced to British gardens by Victorian entrepreneurs was guano, which was discovered to contain a high

Lilies, illustrated here in Robert Thompson's *Gardener's Assistant* of 1886, were introduced from Asia to British gardens by plant hunters in the early nineteenth century. Unusual and decorative plants were collected and displayed in glasshouses and conservatories.

Advancements in the understanding of soil fertility prompted a demand for fertilisers and manure, and companies began to specialise in the supply of manure to gardeners.

concentration of nitrates. Deposits of bird droppings had collected to depths of several metres on undisturbed coastlines with low rainfall which were home to mass colonies of sea birds. Substantial deposits had been discovered in South America at the beginning of the nineteenth century; by

the 1840s deals had been made with the Peruvian government and guano began to be extracted and imported to Britain. Fortunes were made from the sale of guano, and it was seen by many gardeners as a miracle product. High in nitrogen, it was significantly more potent than farmyard manure and was an instant success, supported by the gardening and agricultural press. The international demand for Peruvian guano was met by hundreds of ships onto which barrow-loads of deposits were piled. Within ten years, the supply was exhausted. Governments tried to source alternative deposits to maintain supply, and gardeners turned to artificial fertilisers to meet their requirements.

Cross-pollination of plants had been observed in the wild, and the early hybridisers had experimented by placing the pollen from one plant onto the stigma of another. As fertile seeds were raised, the possibility was explored

Guano was regarded by gardeners as a miraculous fertiliser, and supplies from South America were soon used up. Alternatives were trialled, such as canary guano, the attributes of which are described in this advertisement from 1897.

of selecting certain favourable characteristics from each parent plant. The Victorians used their new scientific knowledge of plant reproduction to breed hybrids with improved vigour, size or colour, manipulating nature according to the desires of mankind. Plant hunters were bringing back seeds and specimens from abroad, and nurserymen brought several new species into cultivation, many of which were then 'improved' to suit the British climate or to meet the fashions of the day. Flowering plants such as begonias and petunias were introduced and promoted for

This award-winning guano, advertised in 1896, derived its potency from fish.

21

Right: Chrysanthemums were a popular flower with many Victorian gardeners and enthusiastic collectors delighted in the variety of shapes and colours created by hybridisation.

Below: As techniques of hybridisation became more sophisticated following advancements in the understanding of plant physiology, many new rose cultivars were introduced to fulfil the growing demand for variety in colour, scent and form.

Below right: The unusual flowers and exotic appearance of orchids made them highly collectable and species collected from the wild were extensively hybridised.

Rosiers hybrides remontants.
1. Marguerite Lecureux Fraipont . 2. Noisette Eudoxie.

Cypripedium.
1. C. atsmori . 2.C. pubescens . 3. C. spectabile.

their use in bedding schemes, the nurseries offering a limited palette of colours, marketed to accord with the taste for brightly contrasting hues. The Victorians delighted in the new cultivars of roses and chrysanthemums being created, and by 1840 there were over five hundred different cultivars of dahlia to choose from. Orchids became popular with collectors after the introduction of tropical species in the nineteenth century, and many new cultivars were propagated after John Dominy successfully raised the first hybrid at the Veitch Nursery in 1856.

The advances in scientific understanding were matched by a boom in invention. The pages of gardening magazines were crammed with advertisements for a proliferation of novel gadgets to satisfy the burgeoning market for gardening products. Gardeners could choose from labour-saving spray pumps, patented sunshades and hail protectors, fumigators to remedy pest problems, cucumber straighteners and melon supporters. Hosepipes made from vulcanised India rubber reduced the need for carrying heavy watering cans and netting protected valuable crops from pest attack.

In the 1830s professional gardener William Barron, improving on earlier, simple tree-moving devices, invented a method for transplanting mature trees where the tree was raised using a screw-jack, with the roots encased in a ball of earth resting on a platform. The success of this technique allowed new gardens to be created with the immediate impact of maturity – a useful social instrument for the nouveau riche – and was used to move large trees

Below left: Victorian inventions, such as this pesticide applicator, were designed to assist in every aspect of gardening, supplying the needs of a growing market.

Below: An advertisement from 1878 illustrates one of the many labour-saving garden tools and gadgets available to the new market of middle-class gardeners.

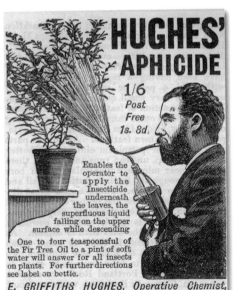

HUGHES' APHICIDE

1/6
Post Free
1s. 8d.

Enables the operator to apply the Insecticide underneath the leaves, the superfluous liquid falling on the upper surface while descending

One to four teaspoonful of the Fir Tree Oil to a pint of soft water will answer for all insects on plants. For further directions see label on bottle.

E. GRIFFITHS HUGHES, Operative Chemist, VICTORIA STREET, MANCHESTER.

THE PERFECT WATERING CAN.
REGISTERED ACCORDING TO THE ACT.

THE PERFECT WATERING CAN.
Registered according to Act of Parliament, and parties infringing will be duly proceeded against.

The advantages this Watering Can possesses over the old kind in use are :—
First.—By having an increased perforated surface the water is more easily distributed. *Second.*—A bed fifteen feet in diameter can be watered with the greatest ease without treading on the soil or having to lift the Watering Can an extra height. *Third.*—The watering can be done in half the time and with half the usual exertion required. They are made of strong zinc and will last a life-time. PRICES—No. 1, 1 Gallon, 5s. 0d. ; No. 2, 2 Gallons, 6s. 6d. ; No. 3, 3 Gallons, 8s. 6d. ; No. 4, 4 Gallons, 10s. 6d.

There are two tubes sent with each Can, one for watering wide and large plots, as shown, the other for particular pots or rows.

The first lawnmower, patented by Edwin Budding in 1830, illustrated in Loudon's *Encyclopaedia of Gardening*.

The successful transplantation of large trees demonstrates the supreme confidence of the Victorians. In this instance, George Jackman, from Woking in Surrey, uses a transplanting machine similar to the one invented by Barron, c. 1914.

as well as topiary specimens. At Elvaston Castle in Derbyshire, where Barron was head gardener from 1830 to 1856, several ancient yew trees were moved distances of twenty-five miles or more to be incorporated into the garden, where they were admired for their unusual forms, peculiar growth patterns and great age, as well as for the remarkable manner of their arrival. In 1880, Barron created publicity by undertaking to transplant an ancient and distorted yew tree, said to be over one thousand years old, growing in Buckland Churchyard in Dover. The tree was successfully moved to a more suitable site in the churchyard, allowing for the extension of the church building, and Barron's feat of botanical engineering neatly demonstrated the confidence of the Victorian innovators to whom anything was possible.

One of the most significant innovations in gardening was the lawnmower, patented by Edwin Budding in 1830. Developed from the nap-cutting

The gardener pushing this lawnmower at Arundel Castle is being assisted by a horse pulling from the front. The early mowers were too cumbersome to be operated easily by one person.

The invention of the mower replaced the laborious job of cutting grass with a scythe, and enabled a smooth and even surface to be achieved with relative ease, popularising the lawn as a garden feature.

An advertisement indicates how technological improvements resulted in mowers which could be operated with ease, including ride-on mowers pulled by horses, designed for use on sports fields.

The invention of the lawnmower revolutionised middle-class gardens by popularising the lawn as a garden feature and encouraging amateur gardeners to mow their own lawns for pleasure and exercise.

The lawn became a characteristic feature of suburban gardens following the introduction of mowers, which could be operated by the amateur gardener (c. 1900).

machine invented to mechanise the woollen industry, it was not merely another ingenious Victorian gadget: this simple device brought new possibilities to gardeners, allowing amateurs to tend their own gardens and promoting the lawn as a garden feature available to all, from stately home to suburbia.

Until the introduction of the lawnmower, grass was cut using a scythe; large areas were worked by a team of men, who rose early in the morning to cut the grass while it was wet. The work was laborious and poorly paid and was considered among the lowliest of garden tasks. The early lawnmowers were made of cast iron with a roller at the back and a cylindrical cutting blade at the front, and the grass clippings were collected in a projecting metal tray as the machine was pushed along. For ease of operation, the mower was fitted with an additional handle at the front to enable it to be pulled as well as pushed. By the 1840s horse-drawn mowers were being used, but further refinements to the original hand-operated design resulted in a device which could be successfully managed without assistance, and they were manufactured commercially from the 1860s. Affordable and easy to use, they were marketed to the aspiring middle-class gentleman and lady amateur gardeners.

A photograph of 1880 shows a conservatory full of attractively arranged exotic plants, displaying the fashionable tastes of the owners.

Just as the invention of the lawnmower stimulated the popularity of the lawn as a garden feature, so the development of cast iron and sheet glass created a demand for glasshouses. The technology to heat a glasshouse efficiently and effectively using a coal-fired boiler and a system of hot water pipes opened up all sorts of possibilities for the cultivation of new plants. Conservatories displaying exotic palms, orchids and ferns became fashionable additions to houses, and public parks and botanic gardens featured magnificent glasshouses exhibiting rare and interesting plants. Kitchen gardens boasted separate glasshouses for the cultivation of vines, peaches and pineapples, and nurseries were able to cultivate new species of plants to meet the growing demand for the exotic, colourful and unusual.

Glasshouses were also used to grow potted plants which were then displayed in the drawing room until they had passed their prime and were returned to the glasshouse to recover, being replaced by another specimen in peak condition. The practice of displaying cut flower arrangements in the house was not popularised until the 1860s. Foliage plants and ferns were fashionably displayed indoors in the protective setting of a Wardian case.

The glasshouses in the kitchen garden were arranged in a more utilitarian style, as at Terregles Garden in Dumfries, c. 1870.

These sealed glass cases provided a self-sustaining environment for plants, where water transpired from the leaves during the day, condensed on the glass overnight, and dripped down onto the soil to be absorbed again through the roots. The case was pioneered by Dr Nathaniel Bagshaw Ward and was described in his book, *On the Growth of Plants in Closely Glazed Cases*, published in 1842. His invention, although not initially designed for ornamental use, gave rise to the craze for ferns and the fashion for the indoor display of plants with interesting foliage, as recommended by Shirley Hibberd in his book *New and Rare Beautiful-Leaved Plants* of 1870. Various forms of the case were produced for ornamental display, including designs imitating the shape and construction of conservatories, with some featuring miniature rockworks and other scenery.

The Wardian case played its part in promoting the novelty of indoor plant displays, but its real impact was more profound. From the 1830s, the Wardian case gave plant hunters a viable means of transporting the living plant specimens collected on their expeditions. Now that more of the plants were surviving the long sea voyage back to Britain, the choice of plants available to gardeners increased, as did the possibilities of introducing economically important plants to distant parts of the Empire. The tea plant discovered growing in China was taken to India where it was successfully cultivated and traded around the world, bananas and rubber plants were introduced to countries with a suitable climate, and the cinchona tree from which quinine is produced was brought from South America to developing countries where it could be used to treat malaria. Advancements in horticulture were having a profound effect on gardens, agriculture, society and the economy.

The Wardian case was invented to facilitate the transportation of live plant specimens, providing a self-sustaining environment, but it also became popular for the indoor display of foliage plants and ferns.

An illustration from *Fern Paradise* of 1878 shows how the basic principle of the Wardian case was adapted for ornamental use, the design taking a more decorative pyramid shape.

29

THE AMATEUR GARDENER'S CALENDAR

BY MRS LOUDON

SPRING

SUMMER

AUTUMN

WINTER

LONDON: FREDERICK WARNE & CO.

SPREADING THE WORD

THE MECHANISATION of the printing process and the abolition of the tax on paper in 1861 made journals, newspapers and magazines an increasingly popular means of disseminating information, and the popularity of gardens, particularly among the educated middle classes, created a demand for gardening publications which had never previously existed. Horticultural journalism was an emerging profession, and writers published their knowledge and opinions on matters of practical gardening, garden style, plantsmanship and garden history.

Garden literature was available before the nineteenth century, including Francis Bacon's *On Gardens* dating from the early 1600s and Philip Miller's *The Gardeners Dictionary* of 1731, but these books did not have the mass-market appeal of the Victorian publications, nor the popular following of avid amateur gardeners. The most important and influential garden book of the nineteenth century was John Loudon's *Encyclopaedia of Gardening*, published in 1822 and reprinted into the 1870s, being updated as the science and practice of horticulture progressed. John Loudon (1783–1843) was a well-respected and influential horticultural journalist who championed the working rights of professional gardeners and offered practical advice and horticultural expertise to aspiring amateurs.

The Gardener's Magazine was founded by Loudon in 1826 as a monthly publication with the intention of spreading knowledge and practical information about gardens and gardening to all who had an interest in the subject. *The Gardener's Magazine* was soon joined by other horticultural, botanical and floristry periodicals established in the 1830s and 1840s. Among them was *The Gardener's Chronicle*, a weekly publication founded by Joseph Paxton and John Lindley in 1841, which was to become the leading horticultural magazine of the Victorian era, respected by working gardeners and amateurs from all classes of society. *The Journal of Horticulture* was another quality periodical, begun in 1848 as *The Cottage Gardener*, but rebranded in 1861 to reflect more closely the social status of its readership. In 1858, the prolific horticultural writer Shirley Hibberd found popular success in his

Opposite:
The Victorians created a burgeoning market for gardening books and magazines aimed at the amateur gardener.

31

Gardening books offered practical advice to amateurs on horticultural techniques, routine garden tasks and choosing suitable plants.

The *Encyclopaedia of Gardening* by John Loudon, published in 1822, was an influential book, respected by professional gardeners and amateurs alike.

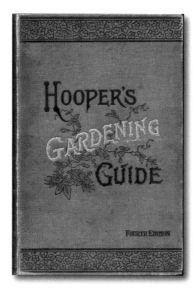

The Amateur's Greenhouse was one of many books written by Shirley Hibberd for the amateur gardener. Hibberd was instrumental in the championing of novice gardeners and believed that a shared interest in gardening could overcome class boundaries.

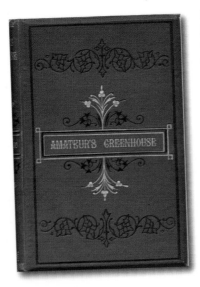

periodical aimed at amateur gardeners, *The Floral World and Garden Guide*, in which he encouraged contributions from amateur gardeners and responded to queries from readers. He published many books offering practical advice on all aspects of gardening, including *The Amateur's Flower Garden*, *The Amateur's Kitchen Garden* and *The Amateur's Greenhouse and Conservatory*, as well as volumes on specific species such as ferns, roses and ivy.

Gardening periodicals served to disseminate the latest horticultural knowledge, promote new plant introductions, offer news and reviews, and advertise the latest products and services. The publication of *The Garden* in 1871 was to herald a move towards the use of periodicals to advocate matters of style and taste in garden design and planting. *The Garden* was founded by William Robinson who used the magazine – along with his later periodical *Gardening Illustrated*, founded in 1879 – to promote his opinions on wild gardening. He also published many books on this theme, the most influential being *The Wild Garden* of 1870 and *The English Flower Garden* of 1883. These publications incited much debate among gardeners and commentators, the most vociferous opponent of Robinson's views being the architect Reginald Blomfield, who published his riposte in 1892 in his book, *The Formal Garden in England*, championing symmetry, straight lines and architectural gardening.

Garden literature provided a forum for debate on horticultural technique and now also on matters of style and taste. Through the letters pages of magazines, everyone with an opinion could have their say, and garden fashions

One of the functions of gardening magazines was the advertisement of horticultural products and services, as illustrated in this page from *Amateur Gardening* of 1899.

Advice from Mrs Beeton extended into the garden, and her popular books were reprinted long after her death in 1865. This version of *Beeton's Every Day Gardening* includes a monthly calendar of garden work.

were shaped more democratically than had been the case in the past when style was generally dictated by the aristocracy. The middle classes were gaining power in gardens as well as in politics and society.

Women gardeners were also now becoming influential. With more middle-class women turning to gardening as a pastime and a means of self-improvement, a market was created for gardening books aimed specifically at women, as well as for tools and gadgets designed for female use. Building on the success of her bestselling *Book of Household Management*, published in 1861, Mrs Beeton compiled a companion volume, the *Book of Garden Management*, which provided the new and inexperienced gardener with all the necessary know-how, from planting and propagation to compost and tools, as well as offering advice on garden layout and suitable trees, shrubs and flowers.

ADIE'S LAWN EDGE CLIPPER.

Cash Price, 10/- each.
Carriage Paid with other Goods amounting to 40/- value.

As more middle-class women became interested in practical gardening, a market was created for tools designed to be used by ladies, as depicted in an advertisement from 1895.

Jane Loudon followed her husband into garden publishing, and through works such as *The Ladies' Companion to the Flower Garden* of 1840, she became the most successful gardening writer of her time. Before her marriage she knew little about gardening, but by assisting her husband with his writing and attending lectures in botany, she built up a wealth of horticultural and scientific knowledge which she then presented to fellow amateurs in books which were accessible and practical.

Jane Loudon also wrote gardening books for children, acknowledging the Victorian expectation of education and improvement in the young. This subject was taken up later by Alicia Amherst, who published *Children's Gardens* in 1903, and Gertrude Jekyll in *Children and Gardens* of 1908. Alicia Amherst is also distinguished as the first writer to publish a scholarly work on garden history in her book *A History of Gardening in England* of 1895.

The widespread appeal of gardening and the Victorian desire to acquire knowledge for self-improvement is demonstrated by

EVERY
LADY HER OWN
FLOWER GARDENER,
BY
LOUISA JOHNSON.
A NEW EDITION

LONDON,
PUBLISHED BY WM S ORR & CO PATERNOSTER ROW.
MDCCCXL.

Garden books specifically for women began to be published in the Victorian era, such as Louisa Johnson's *Every Lady Her Own Flower Gardener* of 1840. The cultivation of flowers was deemed a particularly suitable pastime for ladies.

Victorian children were encouraged to participate in gardening activities, and gardening books were written specifically for children.

the popularity of the many horticultural clubs which were founded in towns and cities around Britain. By the middle of the nineteenth century there were over two hundred gardening societies, the largest of which was the Horticultural Society of London, which was later to become the Royal Horticultural Society.

Founded in 1804, the Horticultural Society had a huge influence on technical developments in horticulture through the trialling of modern methods and new plants. The society employed plant hunters to collect new species from abroad, rather than sponsoring organised expeditions, and ran a horticultural training programme which was highly respected in the gardening profession. In 1822, the Horticultural Society created an experimental garden at Chiswick which became a horticultural hub for training gardeners, trialling plants and developing new techniques.

Gardening shows and competitions organised by societies all over Britain encouraged amateur gardeners and awarded them for their skills.

In the 1830s a programme of horticultural shows was established with competitive classes for flowers and vegetables, giving gardeners a forum for displaying their skills in cultivation and presentation, and the opportunity for recognition among their peers.

The Horticultural Society also played an important role in the correct naming of cultivated plants. A series of meetings was organised in the 1880s to bring together expert knowledge of different species with the aim of

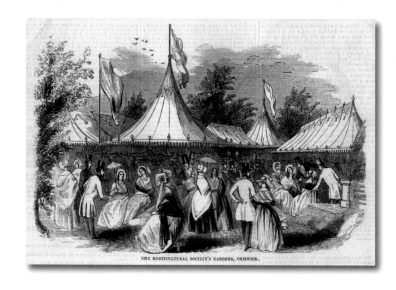

The shows at the Chiswick garden of the Horticultural Society were popular social occasions, as depicted in an illustration from 1840.

THE HORTICULTURAL SOCIETY'S GARDENS, CHISWICK.

identifying and correcting problems in nomenclature, such as regional synonyms. Accordingly, the Apple Congress was held in 1883, followed by the Daffodil Congress in 1884, the Orchid Congress in 1885, and so on.

The society experienced financial difficulties in the 1850s, culminating in the sale of offices, books and drawings. Fortunes rallied when the president, Prince Albert, granted a royal charter in 1861, and the society was renamed the Royal Horticultural Society. In the same year, membership of the society doubled and a new garden was opened in Kensington, laid out in a lavish Italianate style, with terraces, arcades and parterres. Public opinion was divided over the new garden, the expense of which had contributed to the financial troubles of the society, and there was much debate in the gardening press over the choice of the design.

The event which dominated British culture in the mid-nineteenth century was the Great Exhibition, held in 1851 in Hyde Park and attended by over six million people. The exhibition, which showcased British supremacy in design and manufacture and celebrated the achievements of the Empire, was housed in a vast cast iron and glass structure, known as the Crystal Palace, designed by Joseph Paxton and built in just nine months. People marvelled at the size and grandeur of the building, and garden owners were inspired to create their own glasshouses, whether as an impressive setting for the display of palms and orchids or a simple structure for raising seedlings. Inside the exhibition, full-sized trees emphasised the imposing scale of the building and exotic plants formed part of the exhibit.

When the Great Exhibition closed, the building was moved to Sydenham and reopened in 1854 in what became known as Crystal Palace Park. The glass structure was given a magnificent garden setting, with towering jets of water erupting from ponds arranged

When the Crystal Palace was relocated to Sydenham on the closure of the Great Exhibition, the impressive glasshouse continued to instruct and delight the public through displays of exotic plants.

symmetrically around a central avenue with elaborate parterres on either side. Beyond the formal garden was an irregular-shaped lake where a display of life-sized sculptures of dinosaurs exhibited the Victorian advances in evolutionary understanding gained through the discovery of fossils.

The Great Exhibition demonstrated to the nation what had been, and what could be, achieved. The Victorian spirit was one of optimism and

possibility, seen as much in the advancements in horticulture as in the successes of industry and trade. The sharing of this knowledge, skill and enthusiasm spread the appeal of gardening and fuelled the demand for garden products and services. Through books and magazines, horticultural shows, gardening clubs, botanical lectures, and visits to parks and gardens, gardening became embedded in the culture of Britain.

Crystal Palace Park, opened in 1854, combined impressive fountains, elaborate parterres and formal symmetry with an educational display of prehistoric creatures.

THE GARDENING PROFESSION

B Y THE MIDDLE of the nineteenth century, gardening was seen as a good profession for a young man to enter, with decent wages, reasonable working conditions and a fair chance of advancement. The head gardener was a respected member of staff, making decisions on the appearance of the garden as well as its maintenance. By the turn of the century, this elevated position was receding as gentlemen owners of smaller estates assumed artistic control of their gardens, and the gardener became once more subservient to the demands and decisions of his employer.

The employees in large gardens were divided into departments in the same manner as the house staff, with gardeners assigned to a particular area of work. Just as the housekeeper reigned supreme in the kitchen, pantry and scullery, so the head gardener commanded the pleasure grounds, kitchen garden and glasshouses. The hierarchy of domestic servants was reflected in the roles of the gardeners, from garden boy to apprentice, journeyman, foreman and head gardener. A large garden could employ upwards of fifty gardeners in the prosperous era of the mid-nineteenth century, with numbers reducing towards the end of the century as incomes from land fell with the agricultural depression.

The garden boy was the youngest and least skilled member of the garden staff, employed in washing pots and raking leaves, before gradually taking on more responsibility as he learned skills from his superiors. By the age of eighteen, a promising gardener could be apprenticed to a head gardener and would be expected to supplement his practical skills with personal study of botany and horticultural science. Progressing to the position of journeyman gardener, a young man could specialise in a particular aspect of horticulture, such as the cultivation of fruit or exotic plants. The foreman managed other garden staff as part of his role and, by the age of thirty, the most ambitious workers could move on to become a head gardener, directly responsible to the owner of the estate.

Apprentice and journeyman gardeners were provided with free accommodation in the garden bothy, where a woman was employed to cook

Opposite:
Gardening was regarded by the Victorians as a respectable profession with good prospects.

their meals, and do the washing and cleaning. At this stage in their career, employees were not permitted to marry, but progression to the position of head gardener brought with it a cottage where the incumbent could settle with his wife and family. The head gardener was expected to remain at a garden for several years, and a suitable candidate for this important position was often secured by recommendation from another estate. In the 1860s gardening periodicals began to print advertisements for garden staff, indicating the importance of appointing a competent head gardener.

Throughout the nineteenth century, conditions improved for gardeners, and working rights were championed by social reformers. From the 1820s John Loudon campaigned for improved working hours and better accommodation for gardeners and for payment commensurate with education, skills and experience. Loudon was determined to raise the social standing of professional gardeners and afford them the recognition he believed they deserved. In the pages of his *Gardener's Magazine* he brought to public attention the inadequacies of the pay and conditions of many hired gardeners, and highlighted the discrepancies in wages of indoor and outdoor staff, with gardeners being paid substantially less than domestic servants, regardless of training or expertise. Despite gradual improvements in pay and

The garden boy, pictured in the centre of this photograph, would be expected to learn horticultural skills from his superiors and work his way up the profession.

conditions, the Victorian working classes were still expected to put in long hours in the service of their employers. By the end of the nineteenth century, gardeners typically worked ten hours a day for six days a week and were then expected to do further duties on Sunday without pay. Holidays amounted to three feast days a year.

The welfare of retired gardeners and their families also came to the attention of the Victorian social reformers, with the establishment in 1839 of the Benevolent Institution for the Relief of Aged and Indigent Gardeners and Their Widows. Whereas gardeners in private service would usually be provided for on their retirement, jobbing gardeners were faced with the prospect of the workhouse when they could no longer find employment.

For those talented and ambitious gardeners who managed to rise through the ranks to the position of head gardener, status brought with it respect and social standing. The career of Joseph Paxton illustrates the degree of elevation possible through gardening in the Victorian era. Paxton began his horticultural career aged fifteen as a garden boy; by his death in 1865 he had been knighted, was an elected member of parliament, and a wealthy man. After working at the Horticultural Society garden at Chiswick, Paxton was appointed head gardener at Chatsworth at the age of just twenty. His employer, the Duke of Devonshire, had the money and enthusiasm to match Paxton's genius, and the gardens at Chatsworth were

This spacious cottage was provided for the head gardener at Levens Hall in Cumbria, indicating his position as an important and respected member of staff.

A gardener not employed on a private estate had to make a living as a jobbing gardener, advertising his services to find work.

THOMAS HOLLAND,
LANDSCAPE AND
DAY GARDENER,
ASPHALTER, &C.,
HALL STREET,
Moston Lane.

Orders Promptly Attended to.

Joseph Paxton (1803–65) began his career as a garden boy and quickly rose through the ranks to become head gardener at Chatsworth where he created an impressive and celebrated garden, achieving fame and, ultimately, great wealth.

The gardeners at Chatsworth pose in front of the Lily House, designed by Paxton to house a specimen of the enormous water lily, *Victoria amazonica*, raised from a seedling in 1849 and the first to flower in Britain.

embellished in extravagant style. Paxton gained an international reputation, and a knighthood from Queen Victoria, for the design of the Crystal Palace, and he also gained recognition as an architect of country houses and designer of public parks. He wrote gardening books and edited magazines, and was one of the founders of the leading horticultural periodical, *The Gardener's Chronicle*. Paxton was elected Member of Parliament for Coventry in 1854, holding office until his death in 1865, and amassed a personal fortune through investment in railways.

Paxton was an example to gardeners of what could be achieved, and his influence brought new respect to the profession of head gardener. Through

the creation of celebrated gardens and the publication of books and articles, other head gardeners made a name for themselves in the Victorian era and gained the respect of their peers. William Barron was head gardener to the Earl of Harrington at Elvaston Castle in Derbyshire from 1830 to 1865, where he created a garden incorporating spectacular topiary and rare trees. When the garden was opened to the public in 1851 it fuelled much interest in the gardening press, and Barron received recognition for his innovative methods of transplanting mature trees, resulting in the publication of a treatise on his work and further demand for his specialist techniques.

Also highly influential in the development of garden style was George Fleming, head gardener at Trentham from 1841, who created spectacular displays of bedding plants to fill its elaborate parterres. At the same time, Donald Beaton was experimenting with hybridised plants and colour

The bedding system allowed head gardeners to exert artistic control through the choice of colours, pattern and layout. A new scheme could be used each year, giving variety to the owner and a challenge to the gardener. This is Victoria Park, London, c. 1870.

combinations in the bedding at Shrubland in Suffolk. Both gardens were well known, having received acclaim in the gardening press, and Fleming and Beaton were recognised for their influence and innovation in horticulture and garden style. The popular use of bedding in gardens also had the effect of presenting the head gardener with more scope for taking artistic control, as the appearance of the garden could be changed each year with a new bedding scheme embracing different colours and planting combinations.

Gardeners delighted in the new opportunities available for them to achieve glory in their gardens. Whether through skilled use of bedding or the raising of rare and exotic new plants, rewards could be found through personal satisfaction, peer recognition or national acclaim. The competitive spirit of Victorian gardeners is evident in the popularity of horticultural shows. Such events gave gardeners a public platform on which to demonstrate their superior horticultural expertise through award-winning exhibits of flowers and vegetables, and medals were awarded to new plant introductions and hybrids brought into cultivation, bringing instant commercial success to the nurserymen who raised them.

Head gardeners on large estates were also expected by their employers to engage in a game of one-upmanship with neighbouring estates in the cultivation of exotic and unusual fruit and vegetables. To serve a home-grown

Gardener John Hill proudly displays his many awards for horticultural achievement in this photograph of c. 1905.

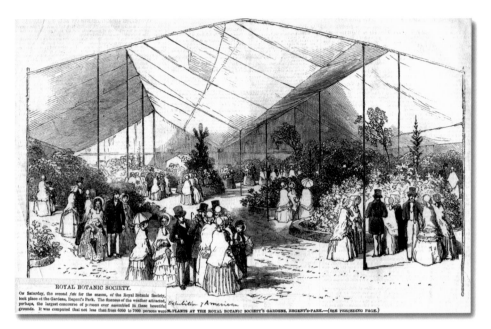

ROYAL BOTANIC SOCIETY.

On Saturday, the second *fete* for the season, of the Royal Botanic Society, took place at the Gardens, Regent's Park. The fineness of the weather attracted, perhaps, the largest concourse of persons ever assembled in these beautiful grounds. It was computed that not less than from 6000 to 7000 persons were **PLANTS AT THE ROYAL BOTANIC SOCIETY'S GARDENS, REGENT'S-PARK.—(SEE PRECEDING PAGE.)**

pineapple or an out-of-season melon, or to display a floral bouquet at Christmas, was an impressive indication of power and status, the glory reflecting on the head gardener as well as his aristocratic employer.

Formal recognition of achievement in horticulture was bestowed through the awarding of medals. In the 1870s the Veitch Memorial Medal was first conferred for outstanding contributions in the science and practice of horticulture, and in 1897 the Royal Horticultural Society established the Victoria Medal of Honour, awarded to those deserving special honour in acknowledgement of their work. Awards of this kind were popular across Britain, and gardeners also competed for horticultural acclaim at competitive shows, the most prestigious events being in London. The Royal Botanic Society's shows at Regent's Park drew large crowds, as did the Crystal Palace Flower Show and the Horticultural Society's shows at Chiswick.

Although most gardeners learned their trade from the practical example of their more experienced superiors, horticultural training courses were becoming available for young students. The Horticultural Society was accepting trainees from the 1820s at its garden in Chiswick, including the young Joseph Paxton. Applicants had to have some experience of gardening, together with a basic education in reading and writing, and had to be unmarried and between eighteen and twenty-six years of age. The training gradually became more formalised, and by 1865 examinations were set. Training was also available at the Royal Botanic Society garden at Regent's

The Royal Botanic Society's American Flower Show of 1850, depicted here in the *Illustrated London News*, showcased the new species being introduced from abroad.

Many middle-class Victorian women were interested in practical gardening on an amateur level, but they were not at liberty to become professional gardeners until the end of the nineteenth century.

Park from the 1840s, where William Robinson began his horticultural career. The Botanic Gardens at Kew formalised their training programme in 1859, and also provided a reading room, which was made available for evening study. Gardening manuals aimed at improving the scientific and horticultural knowledge of professional gardeners were published, including *The Theory of Horticulture*, written in 1840 by the eminent botanist John Lindley. A later edition of the book, entitled *The Theory and Practice of Horticulture*, recorded much better sales among professional gardeners, many of whom were still sceptical of science and preferred to trust the wisdom of practical experience.

A group of female horticultural students at Glynde College are shown with the tools of their trade in this photograph from c. 1910.

Nurseries were established all over Britain to meet the increasing demand for plants, particularly in the south-west where the mild climate produced favourable growing conditions.

Women were employed in the nineteenth century as casual labourers in gardens, doing menial work such as weeding with very poor pay and conditions. As the century progressed, more middle-class women became interested in botany and horticulture, but they were not permitted to apply for any formal training courses until 1891, when places were made available for horticultural study at Swanley College in Kent. By 1895, female gardening staff were employed at Kew Gardens, where they were instructed to wear the bloomers, stockings, boots and peaked caps of their male counterparts, prompting ridicule in the popular press.

As the demand for plants grew, and more and more new varieties became available, nurseries were established around Britain, selling plants through catalogues and at their showrooms and display gardens. Seeds could also be purchased by catalogue, the first produced by Thompson of Ipswich in 1855, and advertisements for seed merchants such as Sutton & Sons were appearing in horticultural magazines by the 1850s.

Seeds were sold through nursery catalogues, with more varieties available to gardeners every year.

COMET ASTER. No 4. 6 vars: for 2/6. page 71.

Carters "TESTED" GARDEN SEEDS. 1898.

JAMES CARTER & Co., 237, 238 & 97, HIGH HOLBORN, LONDON.

In the early years of the Victorian era, the largest and most significant nursery was Loddiges of Hackney, where the collection of palms, orchids and ferns was displayed in a vast ornamental glasshouse, and an arboretum was laid out alphabetically, showcasing the new species of trees available. The nursery was responsible for the introduction of many new species from abroad, and public interest was so great that

Loddiges' *Botanical Cabinet* was published to depict the many new species of plants introduced from abroad. The publication ran to twenty volumes and contained over two thousand plates, including this illustration of a begonia.

An illustration from a supplement issued with *Sutton's Amateur Guide in Horticulture*, c. 1900, showing some of the popular new flower and foliage plants which were grown in bulk by the nurseries and sold at an affordable price to amateur gardeners.

coloured engravings of these new plants were published in several volumes entitled *The Botanical Cabinet*. When the nursery closed in 1854, the collections were sold, with the rarer specimens offered at auction, and many of the palms and exotic plants were bought by Joseph Paxton for display in the Crystal Palace, newly reopened at Sydenham.

The Veitch nursery was established in Exeter by John Veitch in 1808, the premises being expanded by his son James in 1832. To reach a wider audience and compete with other London firms, the nursery opened a showroom in the capital in 1853, taking over the premises of the Royal Exotic Nursery in Chelsea. The nursery in Exeter was retained, along with new premises in Kingston, Slough and Feltham, where the plants were trialled and raised before being brought to London. The success of the Veitch nursery rested on the introductions of new and rare plants from abroad. While there were many wealthy plant collectors willing to pay a high premium for unusual specimens, James Veitch recognised that there was also a market for new plants among middle-class gardeners, and he sought to gather enough seed to raise large quantities of popular new plants in his nurseries which could then be sold on relatively cheaply to meet public demand.

Rather than subscribing to existing plant collecting expeditions, Veitch realised that to meet the demand for novelty, he would have to employ his

The Monkey Puzzle tree was a prized addition to many gardens after it was offered for sale commercially by the Veitch Nurseries, as shown in this photograph from c. 1860.

own dedicated plant collectors. In 1840, the first of these collectors, William Lobb, set sail for Brazil, and was followed in 1843 by his brother Thomas Lobb, who travelled in the east. The firm of Veitch sent out twenty-two plant collectors between 1840 and 1914, and was responsible for the introduction to Britain of a vast number of plants. One of the first packages sent back to

The magnificence of the Wellingtonia, illustrated in James Anderson's *Practical Gardener* of 1880, appealed to the Victorians and the tree was widely planted in arboreta after it was introduced in 1853.

Britain by William Lobb contained over three thousand seeds of *Araucaria araucana*, the Monkey Puzzle tree. This was not a new introduction, but it was a rare and much sought-after plant in Britain. Veitch was able to cultivate a substantial stock of this unusual specimen and within a year was advertising plants for sale. Further commercial success was brought with Lobb's introduction from California in 1853 of *Sequoiadendron giganteum*, the towering redwood which became known as the Wellingtonia. In the course of his career with Veitch & Sons, Lobb was credited in the *Botanical Magazine* with the introduction of one hundred plants.

The new plants brought back from abroad were veiled in secrecy until they were officially introduced: at the London showroom of Veitch & Sons, the door handle of the New Plant Department was removed to prevent unauthorised access. The plants had to be trialled to ensure they were healthy and would survive the British climate, and the new introductions were not released until the nursery had sufficient stock to meet public demand. Many of the plants sold by the nurseries had been manipulated by skilled hybridists to improve their hardiness and vigour, or crossed with another plant to produce a new cultivar. When the new plants had been named, they were

The introduction by plant hunters of many new species of rhododendron resulted in a craze of collecting, with nurseries such as Knaphill Nursery in Surrey specialising in the sale of rhododendrons.

AZALEA.
Reine blanc Bismarckii.

The many colours and forms of rhododendrons and azaleas appealed to Victorian collectors, and the variety available was greatly increased by hybridisation.

introduced to the gardening public on trade stands at horticultural shows, in illustrated articles in the gardening press, and through advertisements.

The plant hunters who made such a significant contribution to British horticulture were solitary and determined men, often suffering much hardship in the pursuit of plants. Little was known in the Victorian era about many of the countries they were travelling to, and the plant hunters would be unaware of the terrain they were likely to encounter, the variations in temperature they would experience, or the inherent danger from wild animals and bandits. Publications were available with information on geography and foreign customs, but these were invariably inaccurate, superficial or out of date. Many plant hunters endured physical suffering on their expeditions, including Thomas Lobb who lost a leg in 1860 after suffering exposure in the Philippines, and David Douglas who nearly drowned in Canada and lost the sight in one eye before being gored to death by a bull in Hawaii in 1834.

Plants had been collected and exchanged by many countries for hundreds of years, but it was the Victorian invention of the Wardian case, together with the demand for novelty and variety by Victorian gardeners, that fuelled the rapid introduction of so many new plants in the nineteenth century. Some of the plant hunters were enthusiastic amateurs, funding their own travels and motivated by a sense of adventure and personal ambition. Others were sponsored by syndicates of wealthy landowners, driven by the prestige of being the first to grow new species of trees in their gardens, or by botanic gardens wanting to increase the diversity of their collections. Joseph Dalton Hooker, who was to become the director of Kew Gardens in 1865, collected extensively in the Antarctic, New Zealand, Tasmania and the Himalayas, and introduced twenty-five new species of rhododendron to Britain, resulting in a ferment of rhododendromania. The Horticultural Society employed plant hunters including David Douglas and Robert Fortune, with the aim of improving horticultural knowledge, and the nursery firms sought commercial reward and novelty by contracting their own dedicated collectors. The plant hunters also played a crucial role in the expansion of the Empire and the British economy by instigating the trading of such commodities as tea, quinine and rubber.

PART TWO

GARDEN STYLE

Fig. 2.

Previous page:
The Pelargonium
Garden at
Chatsworth of
1851 shows a high
level of artifice in
the design, and
celebrates one
of the newly
introduced species
of bedding plants.

Victorian
gardeners began
to appreciate the
variations in
colour and form
found in evergreen
plants, and conifers
were incorporated
into garden
planting as new
species were
introduced
from abroad.

CUPRESSUS (CHAMÆCYPARIS) LAWSONIANA ERECTA VIRIDIS.
(LAWSON'S ERECT CYPRESS.)

As the nineteenth century progressed, artistry began to dominate garden style as the landscape garden gave way to flowers, pattern and structure. The informal landscapes of Lancelot 'Capability' Brown (1716–83) had been designed to imitate nature, creating an idealised landscape setting appropriate for a grand country house. Nature spread out from the front steps as far as the eye could see, the contrast between building and landscape emphasising the grandeur of the architecture, and the whole impression asserting the dominance of the owner. Humphry Repton (1752–1818) eased the transition from architecture to landscape by introducing flower beds around the house, giving added interest from the windows while maintaining the impressive parkland views beyond.

Repton's flower beds were gradually given shape and structure, from the irregular teardrop outlines of the gardenesque to symmetrical layouts and elaborate fretwork parterres. Terraces with balustrades, statues and steps extended the architectural style of the house into the garden, and led to the shrubbery which eased the final transition into the informal parkland beyond.

The grand country houses led the way in garden style, and the new Victorian middle classes sought to proclaim their status by emulating their aristocratic neighbours, albeit on a reduced scale. Aristocratic landowners then began to distinguish themselves from the usurping nouveau riche by reviving ancient garden styles to emphasise their family lineage. They looked to Tudor and Elizabethan gardens and created hedged allées, topiary, knot gardens and mazes, evoking familial associations with the perceived golden age of British history. The middle classes, with no ancestry to celebrate, created cottage gardens in the belief that they were reviving a traditional British way of life, and returning to the simple pleasures of flowers and nature. Victorian gardens became enveloped in pastiche, historic revival having little concern with actual history and more regard to the visual effects that could be achieved. Elements of historic gardens from Britain and abroad were artfully selected and combined before undergoing a Victorian refurbishment using hybridised plants and modern materials.

The new plants which were becoming available to Victorian gardeners influenced garden style by establishing trends and opening up new possibilities of design. In the 1830s, the gardenesque style developed to show individual plant specimens to their full advantage, planted in beds where they could be

CARTERS JAPANESE LANDSCAPE GARDENING.
The GOLD MEDAL AWARD, HOLLAND PARK, 1909.

admired from all angles. The composition of the planting was subservient to the content, and the layout was more reminiscent of a museum than a natural landscape. The gardenesque style was embraced by Victorian botanic gardens and arboreta where collections of plants and trees were displayed to encourage individual study and appreciation. Wealthy landowners who subscribed to plant-hunting expeditions were eager to showcase the new and rare specimens being introduced from abroad, and many large gardens incorporated an arboretum or pinetum, with some laid out according to geography or taxonomy. The popularity of conifers increased as more and more new species were brought into cultivation, with gardeners valuing the winter foliage and variations in form and colour. Conifer avenues became a celebrated feature, with Elvaston Castle in Derbyshire boasting an avenue consisting of parallel rows of Irish and golden yews, Monkey Puzzles, deodars and pines, and the avenue at Bicton Park in Devon was planted entirely with the new and exotic Monkey Puzzle tree.

As the east was opened up to plant collectors, the interest in Japanese gardens developed. By the end of the nineteenth century bamboos, maples and flowering cherries were epitomising in gardens the Victorian enthusiasm for blue and white china and Gilbert and Sullivan's *The Mikado*. The publication in 1893 of Josiah Conder's book *Landscape Gardening in Japan* brought a new understanding of the oriental style of gardening, but the Victorians failed to grasp the essential substance of Japanese garden design, adopting aspects of the outward appearance but not the underlying philosophy.

An advertisement shows the range of features adopted in Britain to create gardens in the Japanese style, including waterfalls, rustic bridges, stone lanterns and statues of cranes.

Overleaf:
The garden at Broadlands was landscaped by 'Capability' Brown in 1767, and illustrates the style of country house garden predominant before the Victorian age.

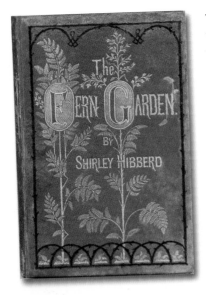

The Fern Garden by Shirley Hibberd was published in 1872 in response to the growing Victorian interest in collecting and displaying ferns.

They selected elements of the Japanese garden – such as waterfalls, rustic bridges, stone lanterns and bonsai trees – and assimilated them into a garden style which was much more Victorian than Japanese.

The introduction of new species of rhododendron in the 1850s prompted a craze for this new and colourful plant, resulting in the exotic embellishment of woodland gardens and giving fuel to the wild gardening movement. Ferns also captured the interest of the Victorians, and were displayed in ornamental Wardian cases in fashionable middle-class drawing rooms or in specially designed fern houses. Books devoted to ferns were published in the 1840s and by the 1860s several nurseries were specialising in the supply and cultivation of ferns and foliage plants.

The new alpine plants being stocked by nurseries inspired enthusiasts to create their own rock gardens, some imitating mountain scenery and incorporating scaled-down versions of the Alps or the Khyber Pass. Rockwork was regarded as a pleasant contrast to the formality of the flower garden, and the rock garden was treated as a distinct garden feature. The most celebrated rock garden of the Victorian era was at Friar Park in Oxfordshire, begun in 1875 by Sir Frank Crisp. The garden featured an Alpine landscape, complete with imitation Matterhorn towering to nearly 10 metres, cascades, ravines, rocky slopes and scree, with a network of caves and a grotto excavated below ground. The

Ferns and collections of foliage plants were suited to indoor display and were housed in ornamental Wardian cases, seen here in an illustration from 1878.

landscape was filled with alpine plants arranged in massed groups amid the rockworks, and cast-iron chamois embellished the scene.

In the early rock gardens, art dominated nature. Large rocks were positioned in circles and archways to emphasise the fact that their arrangement was devised and constructed by the skill of mankind. The rock gardens at Elvaston in Derbyshire, created in 1838, and at nearby Chatsworth, laid out by Paxton in 1842, mix naturalism with obviously man-made elements, incorporating huge rocks, to celebrate the power of their owners. The firm of Pulham & Son began to specialise in creating rock gardens using their own brand of artificial stone made from clinker bound with cement, which became known as pulhamite. They were able to provide rocks and boulders of a consistent colour in any shape and size, resulting in a surprisingly natural effect.

The firm of Pulham & Son specialised in the construction of artificial rockwork, known as Pulhamite, made from clinker and cement and moulded to imitate the natural strata of rock.

Some rock gardens were created within quarry sites, such as at Belsay Hall in Northumberland. Sir Charles Monck created a garden of massive rock faces, ravines, arches and pinnacles in the area where stone had been quarried for his new house in the early nineteenth century. The rock was deliberately extracted in the shape of a picturesque canyon, with the intention that the quarry would become a garden feature, and Scots pine and yews were planted along the top of the cliff to heighten the drama of the scale. Work on the garden was continued in the 1870s by Monck's grandson, the plantsman Sir Arthur Middleton, who added exotic species and hybrid rhododendrons to the quarry. On a similarly magnificent scale was the rock garden at Stancliffe Hall in Derbyshire, created in a sandstone quarry hewn from the hillside in a massive landscape of boulders and outcrops. By the 1870s, rock gardens were huge and bold, with plantings of a compatible scale, providing settings for the new conifers and shrubs coming into cultivation.

The Victorian interest in geology produced rock gardens which combined the display of alpine plants with geological specimens, corals, shells and flints, resulting in a picturesque effect not usually conducive to the growing requirements of the plants. As the nineteenth century progressed, the construction of rock gardens came to be dictated by the needs of the plants rather than the effect of the composition. Rock gardens became flatter and replicated more closely the native moraine habitat from which alpine plants were collected.

The new flowering plants being brought to Britain from South America and South Africa provided the perfect mass of colour needed to enrich the

flower gardens of fashionable Victorians. Nurseries stocked petunias, calceolarias, salvias, lobelias, verbenas and pelargoniums, and hybridists ensured bright colours and healthy, compact plants. Italianate parterres and massed bedding schemes were made possible by these new plants, and colour became a dominant feature of the garden.

By the 1840s a system of massed bedding was developed, using contrasting colours to create spectacular visual effects. Gardeners looked to new ideas in colour theory being introduced to Britain from the continent and experimented with combinations of tone, brightness and contrast. Goethe's *Theory of Colours* was translated into English in 1840 and recommended the use of complementary colours – red and green, blue and orange,

The new introductions of flowering plants from abroad stimulated the fashion for colourful bedding schemes, and hybridised plants increased the variety available. This assortment includes some Victorian favourites.

yellow and violet – as most pleasing to the eye. Practical experiments by gardeners took into account the effect of light and weather, the size of the plants, and the shape of the bed. Ribbon borders with flowers arranged in rows of contrasting colours led the eye along serpentine lines, and pincushion beds of concentric circles were arranged symmetrically along paths.

A bedding design showing an arrangement where blocks of colour are used to create a vibrant pattern of contrasting hues. Other schemes used ribbons of colour within a bed to create patterns.

This style of bedding was embraced by the newly developing public parks, where the bright colours and patterns were popular with the working classes, providing a welcome change from dreary factories and smoke. The parks continued to create impressive displays of massed bedding throughout the nineteenth century and beyond, but by the 1860s the dominance of brightly contrasting hues in private gardens had given way to more subtle colour combinations. Neutral shades and greenery were recognised as important to avoid vivid juxtapositions of colour, and compositions where the tone of a single colour was varied within one bed were considered more tasteful than primary contrasts.

One of the drawbacks of the annual bedding system was the lack of seasonal interest, with beds left bare from autumn through to early summer. In large gardens, the removal of bedding coincided with the annual departure of the family for London, so the absence of flowers went unnoticed, but the gardeners of more modest employers were increasingly looking for ways to extend the bedding season, using spring bulbs and dwarf conifers. Bedding also required a huge amount of effort, from planning the colour scheme and design, to raising and tending the plants, transplanting them into position and removing them at the end of the season, all of which came at a considerable financial cost.

The labour necessary to produce massed bedding schemes, and the levels of perfection attained in their execution, are indicative of the proud Victorian work ethic. The desire for novelty led in the 1870s to the development of

The bedding scheme at Terregles Garden in Dumfries, *c.* 1870, used blocks of massed colour to create bold visual effects, necessitating much effort from the garden staff.

carpet bedding, which was an extraordinary demonstration of horticultural skill and endeavour. Created from the close planting of low-lying plants such as sedum and sempervivum which presented a smooth surface patterned like a carpet, this new style was variously known as jewel bedding, embossed bedding, tapestry bedding, artistic bedding or mosaic bedding. The fashion for carpet beds spread from country estates to suburban gardens and public parks, its popularity escalating after the success of a scheme unveiled at Crystal Palace Park in 1875 which featured realistic representations of butterflies arranged over six beds. There was no limit to the Victorian sense of invention realised through carpet bedding, with complicated patterns incorporating heraldic devices and monograms, zoomorphic designs, portraits and mottos, and three-dimensional works of art in the form of animals, crowns and clocks.

Hundreds of bedding plants had to be raised from seed in the glasshouse before being transported to the garden, where the soil was prepared and individual plants were laid out in position before being planted and watered.

Although some Victorian gardens are seen as the epitome of a particular style, such as the Italianate masterpiece of Trentham or the Arts and Crafts idealism of Red House, others incorporated several styles and features in different parts of the garden. It was not unusual to find a gardenesque shrubbery, a rose garden, a formal parterre, a rock garden and a display of carpet bedding all within the boundary of a single estate, reflecting the eclectic tastes of the owner and an attempt to keep up with changing fashions. Gardens were also extensively accessorised by the Victorians to add character

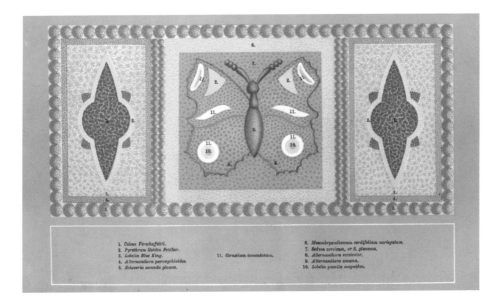

1. *Coleus Verschaffelti.*
2. *Pyrethrum Golden Feather.*
3. *Lobelia Blue King.*
4. *Alternanthera paronychioides.*
5. *Echeveria secunda glauca.*

11. *Cerastium tomentosum.*

6. *Mesembryanthemum cordifolium variegatum.*
7. *Sedum corsicum, or S. glaucum.*
8. *Alternanthera versicolor.*
9. *Alternanthera amœna.*
10. *Lobelia pumila magnifica.*

and display taste. Rustic buildings and garden furniture were popular additions, as were Japanese tea-houses and oriental bridges. Rockeries brought opportunities for imitative landscaping and novel scenery, and in the 1890s gnomes made their first appearance in British gardens.

Some gardens were so eclectic, novel or pioneering in their design, that they defy classification into any established garden style. Regarded as a curious anomaly when it was opened to the public from 1839, the garden at Alton Towers in Staffordshire was created by the fifteenth Earl of Shrewsbury between 1814 and 1827, and was among the most renowned gardens of the Victorian age. The Earl sought advice on the layout of the garden from various experts, including John

The *Gardener's Assistant* of 1888 included several carpet-bedding designs which could be copied by gardeners keen to incorporate the fashion into their own gardens.

Companies specialising in the manufacture of rustic garden buildings, furniture and ornaments were established to meet the popular demand for rustic additions to the garden.

Loudon, then promptly ignored all their recommendations and delved into the fancy of his own imagination, creating a gothic tower, Greek temple, Chinese pagoda, Swiss cottage, and recreation of Stonehenge, as well as an assortment of fountains, grottoes, terraces, conservatories, arbours, bridges and statues. The garden was an eclectic mixture of architectural and garden styles which defined the eccentric tastes of the owner rather than heading a movement in garden design. Although not widely imitated, Alton Towers was nevertheless popular as a Victorian curiosity.

Another garden to receive popular public acclaim was Elvaston Castle in Derbyshire, seat of the fourth Earl of Harrington, laid out between 1830 and 1850. The main feature of the garden was a collection of clipped evergreens and topiary shapes surrounded by a yew tunnel, punctuated at intervals by windows through which to glimpse the extraordinary views beyond. The garden contained early examples of Monkey Puzzle trees, and other rare and unusual trees had been incorporated into the garden as fully grown specimens by head gardener William Barron, using his transplanting machine. An arboretum had been stocked with many of the new conifers introduced from abroad, and there were magnificent avenues, a lake and a rock garden. The garden was little known until it was opened to the public in 1851, when it was widely visited for its novelty and peculiarities.

Gnomes were
introduced to
Britain from the
continent in 1890,
and became a
curiosity in
Victorian rock
gardens.

The garden at Biddulph Grange in Staffordshire, created in the 1850s by James Bateman, was innovative and eclectic in style yet highly influential in layout. Bateman laid out a series of separate gardens, each ingeniously linked to unify disparate elements while avoiding visual contrasts. The plants used by Bateman were given an appropriate geographical setting and themes of history and geology were explored in a layout reminiscent of the courts at the Great Exhibition. The garden featured an Egyptian Court, entered through a yew pyramid flanked by sphinxes, which led through a dark tunnel to a Cheshire cottage and then into a pinetum. A cave in a landscaped 'Scottish' glen led by a flight of stone steps to 'China' where a section of the Great Wall had been recreated along with a temple and a statue of a dragon. Each of these incongruous elements was screened from the next, creating a clandestine garden of concealment and discovery, designed in complete contrast to the monumental prospects and open vistas of the Italianate gardens fashionable at the time.

Thus garden style kept evolving throughout the Victorian era, from open to enclosed, colourful to muted, ostentatious to humble, rejecting nature and informality in the gardenesque and Italianate styles before finally embracing them again at the end of the nineteenth century in Arts and Crafts and wild gardens.

The garden at Elvaston Castle was regarded as a curiosity by Victorian visitors and commentators owing to the unusual layout of enclosed spaces and use of clipped hedges and topiary.

GARDENESQUE

THE WORD 'gardenesque' was first coined in 1832 by John Loudon to express a style of planting in reaction to the picturesque. Loudon believed that rather than imitate nature, a garden should be recognisable as a work of art. He asserted that plants growing within the garden boundary should be allowed to display their true form and character, in contrast to the rugged, wind-swept trees and shrubs competing for light and water to be found in the wild. Loudon advocated the planting of introduced rather than native species to emphasise this departure from nature, and proposed that each plant be positioned to be viewed and appreciated from all angles, rather like distinct and isolated exhibits in a museum. The grass of the lawn should not resemble the grass of the field, and flowers should be planted individually in a bed, separated by neatly raked soil.

Writing in *The Suburban Gardener* in 1838, Loudon explained his theory of demonstrating the supremacy of art over nature, stating that whereas the picturesque was an imitation of wild nature, the gardenesque was 'the imitation of nature, subjected to a certain degree of cultivation or improvement, suitable to the wants and wishes of man.' The resulting effect was a scattered layout of trees and shrubs linked by winding paths, with irregular beds arranged to display each plant as an individual specimen. Trees were often planted on mounds of earth to improve their presentation, and this method was successfully used when transplanting large trees into the garden. The gardenesque principle allowed for the integration of unusual trees, such as the Monkey Puzzle, into a composition where the layout was determined by individual specimens rather than overall effect.

Loudon's carefully considered principles were not fully grasped by contemporary garden theorists, and by 1850 the meaning of 'gardenesque' had become subverted and was being used by garden commentators to describe a garden style rather than a planting principle. The 'mixed', 'middle' or 'irregular' style was a blending of art with nature, somewhere between the formal and the picturesque, and could describe the majority of gardens

Opposite:
The mix of different features and styles, asymmetric layout, and blending of formal with informal in the garden at Castle Coombe in Wiltshire define it as gardenesque, pictured in E. Adveno Brooke's *Gardens of England*, 1856–7.

created in the early Victorian era. Straight lines and symmetry were considered to be too artificial, so paths were winding and the edges of borders curved. Flower beds were circular or teardrop shaped and were positioned at irregular intervals among scattered clumps of exotic trees and shrubs chosen for their distinctive outlines or unusual foliage. The use of variety and colour in the garden mirrored the style which dominated the interiors of Victorian houses, characterised by an eclectic mix of texture, colour and form.

With this new understanding of the word, the gardenesque encompassed mid-nineteenth-century gardens characterised by the artful composition of elements within the design, the isolation of individual plants and the high degree of cultivation maintained. 'Gardenesque' was a label which could be applied to gardens of any size, where a mix of specimen plantings, island beds and garden buildings was linked by serpentine gravel paths. Gardens such as Alton Towers, laid out with an incongruous mixture of garden elements borrowed from various disparate architectural traditions and artistic styles, were described by contemporary commentators in the 1850s as 'gardenesque', indicating how far the meaning of the term had strayed from Loudon's original proposition.

Opposite: This engraving, from the frontispiece of Charles McIntosh's *Practical Gardener* of 1828, illustrates the gardenesque style as defined by John Loudon, where the arrangement of individual specimens determined the composition, and plantings were highly cultivated.

Below: Trees with a weeping habit were incorporated into gardenesque layouts where their unusual forms could be viewed from all angles.

This drawing of 1836 depicts the scattered layout typical of the gardenesque, with irregularly arranged beds in circular and tear-drop shapes, and areas of neatly raked soil separating each plant.

Although gardens began to assume a more formal aspect with the growing popularity of regular flower beds and symmetry, the design of public parks carried forward the gardenesque layout and planting style which suited the requirement for variety and interest. Public parks were laid out with serpentine walks and clumps of trees, each element distinct in character and presentation. Lakes, fountains, massed displays of bedding, rock gardens, rose gardens, glasshouses, sports facilities, bandstands and refreshment kiosks were all incorporated as separate elements in the composition, arranged in the manner in which Loudon might have positioned specimens of exotic shrubs.

Gardenesque principles were also adopted at botanic gardens where the notion of positioning each specimen to be individually studied was already

established. The purpose of such gardens was the study and collection of living plants, displayed according to taxonomic orders. The order beds of the botanic garden complied with Loudon's original gardenesque principles, where plants could be viewed separately to full advantage, and the outer areas of many botanic gardens were laid out with artfully arranged beds displaying scientific collections of plants. Cambridge University Botanic Garden, opened to the public in 1846, was laid out with a serpentine path following the circumference of the garden, around which were grouped taxonomic collections of trees. A broad central avenue separated the lake from the order beds in a gardenesque composition incorporating specimen plantings within a designed landscape.

Dicksonia antarctica.

Many Victorian landowners planted an arboretum in which to display the new species of trees being introduced from abroad, often laid out following gardenesque principles. Some arboreta were landscaped in a picturesque manner with trees arranged such that they could be admired individually, while others grouped specimens according to geographic origin or arranged trees alphabetically. Derby Arboretum, designed by Loudon and opened in 1840, was laid out using the gardenesque method of planting, with two main walks leading among specimen trees arranged individually to grow to full advantage. The arboretum gave Loudon the opportunity to realise his gardenesque principles in an area designed for public access, education and enjoyment.

The planting of exotic specimens, particularly those with interesting and unusual forms, further emphasised the gardenesque principle of art dominating nature by the use of non-native species.

ITALIANATE

Now that flower gardens were beginning to embellish the environs of grand country houses, their owners sought an appropriate style to complement the grandeur of the architecture and the setting. Charles Barry (1795–1860) introduced his Italianate style to aristocratic landowners in the 1840s and this was to dominate the design of country house gardens for the next two decades. With terracing, steps and balustrades, punctuated by urns and fountains, Barry's designs were formal, architectural and geometric, their bold precision complementing the classical orders of the house.

Barry was an architect, designing buildings in the Italian style before becoming known for the gothic magnificence of the Houses of Parliament, completed in 1852. The gardens he created were designed as an extension of the domestic architecture, serving to highlight the grandeur of the building, rather than existing as a separate entity, and as an architect he had little experience of horticulture. He was content to leave the planting of his terraces in the hands of the head gardeners, giving them the opportunity they craved for artistic expression, and the results were bold, bright and colourful. On some commissions, Barry collaborated with landscape architect William Andrews Nesfield (1793–1881), who designed elaborately patterned parterres to ornament the terraces, bringing a new layer of meaning to the term 'Italianate'.

The Italianate garden of the Victorian imagination was very different from the gardens of Renaissance Italy which they believed themselves to be emulating. Italian gardens were symbolic and philosophical, combining ideas of art and nature with the iconography and metaphor of Greek mythology and the ancient texts of Vitruvius and Pliny the Elder. The layout was theatrical, laden with grandeur, humour, sensuality, surprise and symbolism. Italian gardens were designed for the Italian climate, with shaded walks and cooling water. Cypress and citrus trees provided a framework, along with statues and urns, and the colours were restricted to a palette of green and white, enlivened by the Mediterranean sun. Very few Victorians had visited Italy, and those who had would have seen the gardens of the Renaissance,

Opposite:
The steep hillside setting of the garden at Shrubland enabled Barry to create an architectural, terraced landscape in the manner of the great gardens of the Italian Renaissance, portrayed by E. Adveno Brooke in 1858.

77

such as the Villa d'Este at Tivoli, in a state of overgrown decay, far from their former magnificence.

The Victorian idea of the Italian garden was based on a mix of history and imagination. Inspiration was gained from the English gardens of the seventeenth century, created in the Italian style by aristocrats returning from the continent with a desire to display their fashionable taste through garden design. Gardens such as that at Wilton House, designed in *c.* 1632 by Isaac de Caus, were laid out symmetrically with the house placed as the focal point of the composition,

following the regular axial plan of the grand Italian gardens. Features such as terracing, statuary and grottoes were popularised by the Grand Tourists, and were publicised in the writings of John Evelyn, among other seventeenth-century travellers. The Victorian vision of the Italian garden was therefore a revival of an historical style of garden design in Britain as well as a contemporary reinterpretation of the gardens of the Italian Renaissance.

The term 'Italianate' was used as a label to describe the revivalist style which also encompassed the French tradition, becoming popular in Britain

Italianate gardens were architectural, with terraces, steps, balustrades and urns arranged in symmetry with the house, as at Westfield House on the Isle of Wight, pictured in E. Adveno Brooke's *Gardens of England*, 1856–7.

Visitors to Italy would have seen the surviving Renaissance gardens in a state of crumbling decline, as shown in this eighteenth-century engraving of the once-magnificent Villa d'Este at Tivoli.

The parterre at Arundel Castle, photographed in c. 1875, incorporates trees shaped to resemble the citrus and cypresses of Italy, characteristic plantings in Italian gardens to which the British climate was not conducive.

after the Restoration in 1660, and the Dutch style, which had influenced gardens following the Glorious Revolution of 1688, as well as the Tudor knot garden. It was believed that all these garden traditions had their roots in Italy, and therefore the term 'Italianate' was applicable to describe the style popularised by the Victorians. The outcome was a mixture of

continental influences, with recognisable features borrowed from several different traditions before being embellished by Victorian gardeners with brightly coloured bedding plants.

The use of bedding, which became synonymous with the Italianate style, was developed to furnish the parterres laid out on the formal terraces of the Italianate garden. The garden at Trentham, laid out by Barry in 1840–2, was celebrated for the spectacular use of massed bedding by head gardener George Fleming, and did much to popularise both the Italianate style and the

The bright colours of hybridised pelargoniums which formed the massed displays of bedding in Victorian Italianate gardens were a fundamental departure from the gardens of Renaissance Italy.

The garden at Trentham epitomised the Italianate style and did much to popularise the bedding system in Britain, bringing colour to the formal architectural layout. The upper terrace is depicted by E. Adveno Brooke.

bedding system. Barry remodelled the house along Italian principles and transformed a flat expanse of grass into a series of stepped terraces, advancing from the house into the wider landscape in a progression of balustrades, statues, vases and fountains. The upper terrace was arranged around a central circular bed, while the lower terrace featured a broad walk with a rectangular parterre on either side. The garden was embellished with Portuguese laurel trees, clipped to resemble the citrus trees of Italy, and Barry recommended that a gondolier be employed to add an Italianate quality to the lake.

At Shrubland in Suffolk, Barry was presented with a more favourable landscape in which to create an Italianate garden, with a steep slope

A planting plan of 1852 illustrates a bedding design in the form of the French *parterre de broderie*, popularised by William Nesfield.

descending from the house into the parkland beyond, into which he constructed a series of terraces with balustrades, steps and a loggia from 1851–4. Barry was among the few Victorians who had travelled widely in Italy, and his designs were based on the buildings and landscapes he had studied. The garden at Shrubland had all the architectural majesty of the Italian Renaissance, ornamented with the ostentation and flamboyance of Victorian bedding.

Nesfield's parterre at Somerleyton Hall in Suffolk uses gravel to outline a complicated scrolling pattern of bedding, shown in a photograph from the 1860s.

The massed bedding of Barry's terraces evolved into more elaborate designs which further corrupted the true Italian form, coming as they did from the French formal tradition. It was Nesfield, the landscape architect, who was largely responsible for incorporating the parterre into the Italianate garden, and by 1840 he had a thriving business designing parterres for country houses. He began by working in partnership with his brother-in-law, the architect Anthony Salvin, who designed buildings in a revivalist style. Nesfield looked to historical sources in an attempt to create gardens with a character to complement the architecture of the houses, copying the published parterre designs of seventeenth-century French landscape architect Dézallier d'Argenville in his parterre at Worsley Hall, Cheshire in 1846.

Nesfield adopted Italianate terracing and balustrading as a suitable setting for his parterre designs, and became the leading exponent of the Italianate style. His designs were becoming more complicated, taking their inspiration from the French *parterre de broderie*, and by the 1850s he was designing parterres with elaborate tracery patterns, incorporating heraldic motifs and

Nesfield was criticised for his extensive use of coloured gravel in the parterres at the RHS Kensington garden, and the overall design was considered by many to be too architectural.

monograms. This practice served to emphasise the prestige of the owner as well as stamping the mark of British history onto a continental design. Nesfield's parterre designs were in great demand and he worked at large and important estates including Castle Howard, Holkham Hall, Broughton Hall and Witley Court.

Nesfield developed his parterre designs to incorporate the use of coloured gravels, reviving the practice of seventeenth- and early eighteenth-century French and Dutch gardens. The parterres he created for the Kensington garden of the Royal Horticultural Society, opened in 1861, were the epitome of this style, incorporating both gravels and heraldic devices. The Kensington garden represented the culmination of the Victorian Italianate garden and prompted much debate on the horticultural merits of the style. The garden was architectural in character, with terraces, arcades, statuary and ornament taking precedence over plants. Nesfield's parterres were created entirely from box and coloured gravel, incorporating the national motifs of shamrock, thistle, rose and leek. His palette consisted of Derbyshire spa for white, Blue John for purple, Welsh slate for pale blue, pounded red brick for red and pounded yellow brick for yellow, mixing some colours to give intermediate shades and incorporating fragments of coloured glass to catch the light. The colours used were bold and bright enough to rival bedding plants, but it seems the Victorians preferred their gardens to be filled with plants rather than stone dust. The Kensington garden was derided

In 1845 Prince Albert designed an Italianate house and garden at Osborne on the Isle of Wight for the royal family to use as their summer retreat, popularising the style through royal patronage.

for its reliance on architecture and conspicuous lack of plants, and was closed in 1888 when the lease expired.

Despite his many private commissions, and his successful work at Kew Gardens and in the Royal Parks, by the time of his death in 1881 Nesfield's style had plummeted in popularity and his obituaries were brief and reserved. His later work was completed in partnership with his son, Markham Nesfield, including the Italian Garden at Regent's Park, designed in the 1860s with colourful bedding, ornamental vases and clipped hedges arranged along parallel avenues. Although Queen Victoria delighted in the Italianate garden Prince Albert had created for his family at Osborne, she rejected Nesfield's designs for the garden at Buckingham Palace; his elaborate box and gravel parterre complete with royal monogram, fountains and sculptures proved too much for her modest tastes and the scheme was abandoned in 1850.

By the end of the Victorian era, there was a greater understanding of the gardens of the Italian Renaissance through the publication of several books on the subject and the increase in foreign travel. The blend of French, Dutch, Italian and Tudor garden history which the Victorians had discovered in their own historic gardens, embellished with bold colours and hybridised bedding plants and labelled 'Italianate', became a peculiarly British style of garden design, a long way from the symbolic earthly paradise of the Italian Renaissance.

Bowood House in Wiltshire, published in E. Adveno Brooke's *Gardens of England* in 1856–7, depicts the Victorian interpretation of the Italian garden, where the formal architectural layout is embellished with colourful displays of massed bedding.

HISTORIC REVIVAL

IN THE SEARCH FOR A TRUE, historically English style of garden, the Victorians delved into the past to rediscover a time of distinct national character which could be celebrated and revived. The reign of Elizabeth I was seen as a glorious era when Britain ruled land and seas, heroes such as Francis Drake and Walter Raleigh made the nation great, and William Shakespeare composed a cultural legacy to be proud of. Gardens created in the Elizabethan style brought with them the nostalgic image of the respected local squire giving alms to the poor and presiding over the parish, an impression that Victorian landowners were keen to revive.

The Tudor garden of Victorian understanding was a place enclosed by hedges and bowers, with fishponds and fountains, a maze and a mount, featuring a knot garden and clipped evergreens. This impression of history was inspired by illuminated manuscripts and Francis Bacon's essay *On Gardens*, published in 1625. Many Elizabethan gardens had been swept away by the landscapers of the eighteenth century, and those that remained were largely overgrown by the time of their Victorian rediscovery. The romance of these crumbling gardens, redolent of the age of chivalry and heroism, captured the imagination of Victorian novelists, poets and painters. The ivy-clad walls and rose bowers depicted by the Pre-Raphaelite artists demonstrate the desire to return to a golden age in painting as well as in gardening.

Among the old-fashioned gardens to be admired by the Victorians were Montacute in Somerset and Penshurst Place in Kent. These gardens had surviving Elizabethan features and retained the historic character revered in a new era where progress was pushing towards modernity, and stability was to be found in history. By the 1840s, original Tudor gardens were being restored, the results of which captured the Elizabethan character with little regard for archaeology or historical accuracy. At Montacute, where Mrs Ellen Phelips made extensive improvements to the historic gardens from 1840, the original Tudor mount was removed to make way for new terracing in the Tudor style, and a sunken grassed parterre and fountain were introduced, along with clipped yew hedges and avenues. Penshurst Place was restored in

Opposite:
Much of the original topiary at Levens Hall was replanted in the early nineteenth century. By the time Walter Tyndale painted this view in 1886, the topiary was well established, blurring the distinction between new and old.

Overleaf:
This painting by Ernest Rowe of 1893 depicts Montacute House in Somerset where a garden befitting the Tudor history of the house was created from 1840, resulting in the destruction of original features to make way for Victorian revivalist designs.

the 1860s by George Devey, who recreated a series of parterres and enclosed gardens in the Tudor style, using an eighteenth-century engraving from *Britannia Illustrata* for guidance.

The garden at Heslington Hall in Yorkshire was created to harmonise with the Elizabethan architecture of the house, remodelled in a Victorian 'restoration' in the 1850s, here pictured in *Formal Gardens in England and Scotland* by Inigo Triggs, 1902.

Topiary was a distinctive feature of Elizabethan gardens but, as a form of high artistry at odds with the principles of the landscape movement, was deemed deeply unfashionable in the eighteenth and early nineteenth centuries. Few examples of original topiary survived into the Victorian era, and the specimens that withstood the tides of change were generally overgrown and misshapen. At Levens Hall in Cumbria, the garden created in 1694 was preserved by the family throughout the eighteenth century, although the formal structure of the plan was softened by overhanging honeysuckle and trailing roses. The garden, designed by the Frenchman Guillaume Beaumont, included a celebrated topiary garden, as well as a parterre, orchard and bowling green. By the time Mrs Greville Howard

inherited the estate in 1819, the garden was overgrown and in a state of romantic decay. Her head gardener, Alexander Forbes, was instructed to replant nine miles of box hedging to reinstate the formality of the layout, and much of the original topiary was replaced. With this combination of old and new planting within the historic framework of the garden, the lines were blurred between the original character and the restored features.

Many of the gardens praised in the Victorian era for their old-fashioned character were created substantially more recently than was supposed, with topiary adding an air of historic authenticity to a restored garden, and contemporary commentators were fooled into describing them as ancient historic survivals. The garden at Packwood House in Warwickshire was admired for its sixteenth-century features, including a spiral mount, and was renowned for its topiary. By the end of the nineteenth century, the topiary had acquired the characteristics of the 'Sermon on the Mount', with the

The topiary at Levens Hall was laid out in an informal arrangement to the east of the house, pictured in *Formal Gardens in England and Scotland* by Inigo Triggs, 1902.

Topiary, once derided for its artifice, became a celebrated garden feature; 'historic' examples were admired by the Victorians in gardens all over Britain, and were reproduced in books and copied by gardeners.

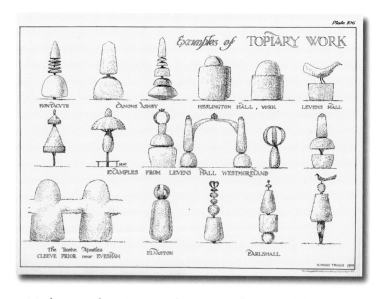

original mount featuring a single yew tree known as 'The Master', surrounded by 'The Apostles' in the form of twelve yews, with four of the larger specimens named 'The Evangelists', and in the lower garden was a further pattern of yews clipped to all shapes and sizes representing 'The Multitude'. Although some of the individual trees may date back to the original planting, it is probable that many of them were introduced in the Victorian era, at which time the topiary was apportioned its biblical significance, adding a further layer of historical intrigue to capture the Victorian imagination. At Hatfield House in Hertfordshire, historical tradition was again fashioned out of yew when, in 1841, a maze was planted in the surviving seventeenth-century garden, which soon became regarded as part of the original design.

By the middle of the nineteenth century, topiary was no longer derided as a garden feature, and geometric shapes began to give a formal structure to garden design, providing an evergreen framework. The simple outlines of cones, cylinders and pyramids soon gave way to more figurative topiary shapes and by the 1870s gardens were adorned with peacocks, crowns, lions and vases. Some enthusiasts took the idea to extremes, creating entire gardens of topiary clipped into spirals, animals, birds, architectural forms and sundials, such as at Friar Park in Oxfordshire and at Ascott in Buckinghamshire. Specialist nurseries were established in response to the demand for topiary specimens, including the aptly named Herbert Cutbush, who promoted his nursery with the slogan, 'Cutbush's Cut Bushes'. Popular opinion on the use of topiary was divided, with public figures including John Ruskin and William Robinson arguing that clipping bushes into unnatural shapes was an abomination, while others published books advocating topiary as an integral feature of the old-fashioned garden. John Sedding's *Garden Craft Old and New*, published in 1891, promoted the use of topiary as a revival of an ancient tradition, and Reginald Blomfield praised the symmetry and precision of clipped evergreens in *The Formal Garden in England* of 1892.

The Victorian interest in old-fashioned gardens was accompanied by a revival of historic styles of architecture, championed by architects including Anthony Salvin who designed new buildings for wealthy clients in his preferred Tudor style, and recommended gardens with an appropriately historical character. Arley Hall in Cheshire, built by George Latham between 1832 and 1845, was created in the Jacobean revival style, and was complemented by an enclosed garden of clipped allées, herbaceous borders and topiary. Whereas the designed landscapes of the eighteenth century were created to harmonise with nature, the revivalist styles of the nineteenth century were intended to harmonise with architecture, bringing a unity to house and garden.

The topiary garden at Friar Park in Oxfordshire mixed geometric shapes with animals and birds, reflecting the eccentric tastes of the owner, Sir Frank Crisp.

ARTS AND CRAFTS

THE ARTS AND CRAFTS MOVEMENT was more a philosophy than a style. Founded in reaction to the relentless progress of industrialisation, Arts and Crafts principles were based on simplicity of design, the revival of traditional methods of craftsmanship and the use of natural, local materials. These principles were expressed through architecture, interior decoration, furniture and garden design, and were embodied in a way of life where purity, innocence, tradition and nature all played an integral role. William Morris (1834–96) was the leading exponent of the Arts and Crafts movement, believing his philosophy to represent a return to a golden age when simple pleasure was derived from beauty.

Morris was inspired by the chivalry of the medieval age and, through his writing, poetry, painting and design, created a fantasy idyll based on Tudor traditions, nature and spirituality. Like the Pre-Raphaelite painters, the poet Tennyson and the architect William Burges, Morris's invocation of an historical golden age represented an escape from the dirt and gloom of industry and the uniformity of mass production. He believed in the aesthetic principle that quality of life could be enhanced by beauty and good design, values which had become overlooked in the industrial age.

The ideals of the Arts and Crafts movement appealed to the middle classes, and the style proved eminently suitable for the small country estates and town houses being built by the newly rich professional classes, satisfying their artistic aspirations and their preoccupation with fashion. Many of the houses and gardens created in the Arts and Crafts manner were underpinned by the irony that their traditional craftsmanship was being paid for with the profits of mass production. Morris's socialist principles were challenged by the fact that only the rich could afford to fill their homes with the handcrafted furniture, textiles and ceramics that his philosophy promoted. Nevertheless, the Arts and Crafts house and garden provided a liberal environment in which the rituals and formality of Victorian society were loosened and progressive thinking was encouraged.

According to Arts and Crafts principles, the architecture of the building, design of the interior and layout of the garden were conceived

Opposite: 'Trellis' was Morris's first wallpaper pattern, designed in 1862, and was inspired by the wattlework fences, climbing plants and wildlife in the garden at Red House.

William Morris
(1834–96), painted
by G. F. Watts in
1870, founded the
Arts and Crafts
movement on his
socialist beliefs.
His principles
are embodied in
his writing, art
and design.

Native plants and
wild flowers, such
as the ox-eye daisy,
were encouraged
in Arts and Crafts
gardens, where
they could spill
naturalistically
over the edges
of flowerbeds.

together in harmony, with the garden plan extending from the house. The inspiration also flowed from the outdoors in, with elements of the garden reflected in the decoration of the interior where flower and leaf motifs were patterned on wallpaper, carved on chimneypieces and forged in metalwork. The building materials used for the house were also used in the construction of garden walls, steps and gazebos, offering a continuity of design. As local materials and traditional craftsmanship were employed, Arts and Crafts houses and gardens were stylistically different from one another, their design depending on regional variations of stone, brick or roughcast, vernacular woodcraft techniques, and the local custom for slate, tiles or thatch.

The planting of the Arts and Crafts garden was accomplished in partnership with nature, guided by art but not controlled by it. In reaction to the vivid massed colours of Victorian bedding plants and the unusual foliage of the exotic species being introduced from abroad, old-fashioned flowers were favoured, such as the hollyhock, convolvulus and rose. The herbaceous border of the Tudor garden was revived, in which the variety of size, shape and colour produced an effect in complete contrast to the uniformity and precision of massed bedding schemes. Design was not imposed on plants; instead the planting choices were informed by the type of soil indigenous to the garden, the aspect of the site and the traditions of the area. Nature was revered, hybridised plants and exotic species were spurned, and plants were encouraged to grow unfettered.

The first garden to embody the ideology of the Arts and Crafts movement was at Red House in Kent, where William Morris lived with his family from 1859 to 1865. The house

Arts and Crafts plantings were made up of old-fashioned flowers which became synonymous with the style, as illustrated in these seed packets of hollyhock and Nigella 'Miss Jekyll' from *c.* 1910.

was designed by the architect Philip Webb, a close friend of Morris who shared his enthusiasm for vernacular designs and traditional methods. From the outset, the design of the building, gardens and interior was conceived as a single entity, with the vision shared between architect and client. The house appears to wrap around the landscape, enclosing a sheltered courtyard on two sides, and was designed to blend into the surroundings. The porch opening onto the courtyard was partly in the house and partly in the garden, integrating one with the other, and the climbing plants wafting their fragrance into the windows of the house also served to blur the distinction between architecture and garden. The plans for Red House are annotated with pencil to indicate the position of plants – including jasmine, rose and passion flower – around the walls of the house, the temporal planting as important to the design as the permanent structure.

The garden at Red House was created within an existing orchard where the fruit trees, arranged along parallel lines, provided a simple structure with paths bordered by lavender and rosemary. On the north side of the house was a formal flower garden divided into four squares separated by rose trellises, creating the sense of an enclosed medieval garden of separate, but linked, spaces. A further trellis ran along the side of the house, connecting the formal garden at the north to the courtyard at the south, which was enclosed by the walls of the house on two sides and by trelliswork on the others. Within the courtyard was a well, constructed from the same brick and

Gertrude Jekyll as photographed in c. 1901 at The Deanery in Sonning, Berkshire, one of the many gardens where she worked in partnership with Edwin Lutyens, blending natural plantings with vernacular architecture.

The house and garden at Red House were conceived as a single entity designed to be unobtrusive in the landscape, as shown in Walter Crane's painting *Tea at Red House* of 1907.

tiles as the house, and designed in harmony with the architecture. The wattlework fences, festooned with flowers, leaves and wildlife, which created the enclosed spaces in the garden, were immortalised in Morris's first wallpaper pattern, 'Trellis', depicting a pattern of flowering roses with birds painted by Webb, designed in 1862. Many other flowers in the garden contributed to the artistic legacy of Morris and his friends in embroidery designs, stained-glass decoration, poetry and painting.

The ideas of William Morris, and the pioneering design principles he had established at Red House, spread in popularity until by the 1880s the Arts and Crafts style was entrenched in the artistic idiom of the middle classes. Gardens were created alongside new country houses for enlightened families, such as the Beales of Standen in West Sussex, whose home was designed by Philip Webb in 1892. Other gardens were designed to harmonise with existing historic houses, as at Great

Tangley Manor in Surrey, begun in 1885. Most gardens were created through a collaboration of architect and gardener, each contributing expertise on matters of design and planting, and often incorporating ideas expressed by the owner.

The most influential partnership between architect and garden designer was that of Edwin Lutyens (1869–1944) and Gertrude Jekyll (1843–1932). Jekyll was a trained artist and designer, skilled in painting, silverwork, embroidery, carving and gilding, who was forced to abandon her artistic career by the age of forty due to her progressively deteriorating eyesight. She was brought up in Surrey and was deeply interested in local rural crafts and traditions and, after meeting Lutyens in 1889, she worked in partnership with him on many projects, including her own home at Munstead Wood.

The garden at Munstead Wood evolved in response to the landscape, and was started several years before Lutyens was employed to design the house, with the architecture blending with the maturing garden as the house was built. Jekyll disregarded the tradition of planting a flower garden in the immediate environs of the house, and instead the principal rooms looked onto a copse of birch trees. Paths bordered with flowers linked areas of the garden, opening up views to the landscape beyond and leading into the nearby woodland. When the collaboration between Jekyll and Lutyens began, structural formality was introduced to parts of the garden at Munstead Wood to correspond with the positioning of the house, and in their later commissions, the layout of the gardens was aligned along the axes of the house.

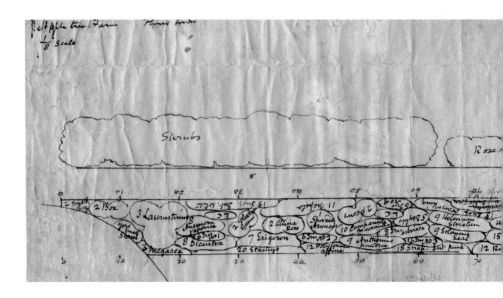

Jekyll's contribution to garden design lay not only in the composition of the garden, but in the colour of the planting. She had studied the work of the colour theorists that proved instrumental in the development of Impressionist painting in France, evident in the paintings of her contemporaries Monet and Pissaro, and adapted the principles to her planting plans. The rules defined by the colour theorists for attaining a harmonious combination of colour applied to painting, and Jekyll realised that the effect of colour in a garden is very different from that on a canvas. The subtle variations of light and weather must be considered, along with the changing perspective of the viewer and the natural growth habit of plants. A colour was not viewed in isolation, but in relation to those surrounding it, as the contrast would affect the true colour of the flower. Therefore, harmonious combinations could only be achieved by an experienced plantsman with a painterly eye. Jekyll's planting plans show a careful gradation of colour, beginning with white at the edges to frame the composition then intensifying towards the centre by gradually blending one shade into the next in drifts of colour to lead the eye smoothly through the design.

The style created in the partnership between Jekyll and Lutyens progressed in popularity into the Edwardian era and beyond, and Jekyll published many books expounding her ideas on planting, colour and garden design. The collaboration between architect and garden designer had effectively combined the traditions of the formal garden with the principles of wild gardening, reconciling two formerly conflicting ideologies.

A planting design by Gertrude Jekyll for the garden at Apple Tree Farm in Hertfordshire, c. 1925, shows her favoured use of drifts of colour blending into one another along the length of the border.

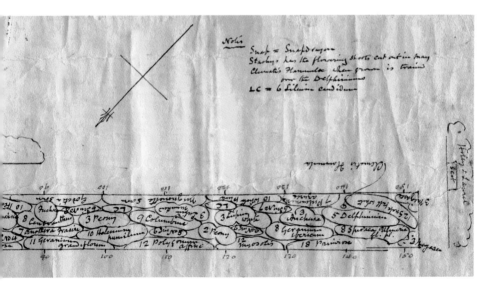

"I wish it to be framed, as much as may be, to a naturall wildnesse."

LORD BACON.

WILD GARDENING

THE PRINCIPLES OF WILD GARDENING were developed in response to the artificiality and formality of the bedding system, and proposed planting in a manner quite opposite to the style of geometric gardening prevalent in the mid-nineteenth century. Wild gardening was not concerned with creating a wilderness or with promoting the exclusive use of native plants, but rather with the embellishment of natural woodland with plants which would add interest and colour, the creation of naturalised wildflower meadows, and the positioning of plants in situations where they would naturally flourish without the need for intervention. Suggestions of these principles are evident from the middle of the nineteenth century in the treatment of outlying areas on some estates and in ideas expressed by garden commentators, but it was William Robinson (1838–1935) who was to give voice to this movement towards informality, expressed in 1870 in his publication *The Wild Garden*. The book prompted a revolution in garden style, at a time when the fashion for architectural gardening was promoting the use of tender plants and massed bedding.

Robinson was born in Ireland, where he learned his trade as a gardener, before coming to England in 1861 and finding work at the Royal Botanic Society's garden in Regent's Park. There he rose to the position of foreman in charge of herbaceous plants, and was responsible for a collection of native wildflower species. Robinson began writing articles for *The Gardener's Chronicle* and within a few years he left the Royal Botanic Society to pursue a career in journalism. He founded his weekly journal, *The Garden*, in 1871, the pages of which became a manifesto for the wild gardening movement and a channel for the promotion of his opinions on garden style. He was a charismatic writer and a vociferous opponent of the fashion for massed bedding, architectural terracing and topiary. He set out his arguments forcefully, his forthright style gaining him enemies while also appealing to the gardening public and bringing his ideas to a wide audience.

In his introduction to *The Wild Garden*, Robinson sets out the reasons for his promotion of this style of gardening, beginning with the fact that most

Opposite:
The frontispiece to the first edition of William Robinson's *The Wild Garden* of 1870 illustrates his gardening principles.

A portrait of William Robinson by Francis Dodd, 1908.

flowers will flourish better outside the flower garden in conditions more suited to their natural habit, where they will also look much better. He observes that the plantings in a wild garden do not suffer visually when one species begins to die back, as the decay is concealed amid vegetation, and the plants can be appreciated for their form and foliage even when not in bloom, unlike in the formal flower garden. Robinson's appreciation of wild flowers is demonstrated by his endorsement of plants which would not be suited to the neat edges of the flower garden, but are nevertheless worthy of cultivation and find a place in natural groupings in the wild garden. He vehemently opposes the bedding system which gives rise to 'the dreadful practice of tearing up the flower-beds and leaving them like new-dug graves twice a year'. His alternative allows for the display of spring bulbs which will naturally die back and be replaced by summer flowering plants without any disruption to the appearance of the garden, or requirement for intervention by a gardener. Lastly, Robinson's principles recommend the inclusion of hardy plants from other parts of the world which add to the interest of the garden without requiring any specialist treatment to become naturalised.

In *The Wild Garden*, Robinson describes the principles of wild gardening and outlines his reasons for promoting the style.

Spring bulbs, such as daffodils, are recommended by Robinson to be planted in huge drifts in woodlands and meadows, where they will naturally die back to make way for summer-flowering plants.

Many of the plants introduced from abroad in the nineteenth century were hardy specimens, able to thrive in the British climate. The principles of wild gardening promoted new plants such as the rhododendron, and the popularity of the plant and the garden style increased simultaneously, with enthusiasts basing the location of their gardens on the suitability of the soil for growing rhododendrons.

Gravetye Manor in Sussex was purchased by William Robinson in 1875. He was able to put his wild gardening principles into practice in the garden and surrounding woodlands.

RHODODENDRON ARBOREUM.

Robinson promoted the planting of hardy non-native plants, such as the rhododendron, which could grow alongside native plants without the need for additional cultivation.

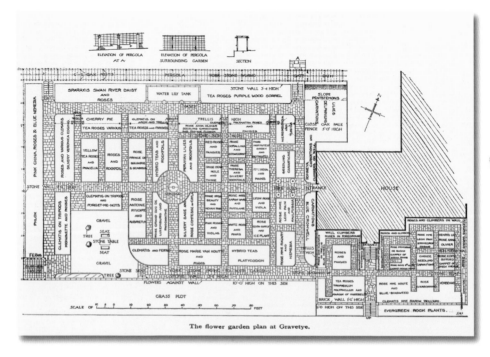

The flower garden plan at Gravetye.

Robinson designed a formal garden next to the house at Gravetye Manor in which his favourite flowering plants were grown, illustrating his view that there was a place for formality in the garden.

A view from the south door of Gravetye Manor looking across the meadow to the lake and woods beyond.

Robinson's aim of planting 'perfectly hardy exotic plants under conditions where they will thrive without further care' was advantageously timed in an era when labour costs were rising and the expense of bedding out large areas of the garden was proving too much for many landowners.

Although Robinson railed against proponents of the formal garden, such as Reginald Blomfield and John Sedding, he did recognise the need for areas of the garden to be devoted to florist flowers, lawns, rockeries and herbaceous borders. He advocated that the wild garden should be allowed to thrive in the outer fringes of lawns, on drives and woodland walks, while others areas of the garden could accommodate such plants as carnations and tea roses, in a setting more formal in character, but where symmetry, uniformity, bedding and topiary were banished. Robinson practised what he preached: his own garden, Gravetye Manor in West Sussex, demonstrated unequivocally the principles of wild gardening as set out in his writings.

Robinson purchased Gravetye Manor in 1885 and lived there until his death fifty years later. The house was Elizabethan but he made no revivalist attempt to harmonise the garden with the existing architecture. Beginning with the removal of the Victorian terraces, rock garden and Wellingtonia plantation, Robinson looked to the landscape to plan his new garden. Much of the estate had been managed as coppiced woodland, providing an ideal setting for Robinson to plant drifts of narcissus and cyclamen, and the woodland glades were embellished with shrubs and clumps of Japanese anemone and trilliums. To the west of the house, Robinson created an area with a formal structure of stone paths and regular flower beds, where the plants were allowed to spill over onto the paths and climb the walls of the house, softening the edges of the geometric outline. Below the formal garden was an alpine meadow where naturalised drifts of spring bulbs gave way to wild flowers in the summer months, and eased the view into the natural landscape beyond.

The garden at Gravetye was indicative of the Victorian reverence for nature, as expressed in the writings of John Ruskin and the poems of William Wordsworth. The ideology of the wild garden allowed nature to flourish in a garden setting and reversed the trend for formality and artifice prevalent in garden design for most of the nineteenth century.

The planting of flowers such as anemone, cyclamen and narcissus was advocated by Robinson to embellish natural woodland.

The wild gardening movement promoted the planting of wild flower meadows, where flowers could grow naturally without the need for cultivation. The Victorians began to appreciate wild flowers, as illustrated in this photograph from c. 1870.

PLACES TO VISIT

Belsay Hall, Castle and Gardens, Belsay, nr Morpeth, Northumberland NE20 0DX. Telephone: 01661 881636. Website: www.english-heritage.org.uk

Biddulph Grange Garden, Grange Road, Biddulph, Staffordshire ST8 7SD. Telephone: 01782 517999. Website: www.nationaltrust.org.uk

Cambridge University Botanic Garden, 1 Brookside, Cambridge CB2 1JE. Telephone: 01223 336265. Website: www.botanic.cam.ac.uk

Chatsworth House, Chatsworth, Bakewell, Derbyshire DE45 1PP. Telephone: 01246 565300. Website: www.chatsworth.org

Crystal Palace Park, Thicket Road, Crystal Palace, Penge, London SE20 8DT. Telephone: 020 8778 9496. Website:"http://www.londontown.com/" www.londontown.com/ LondonInformation/Recreation/ Crystal_Palace_Park

Garden Museum, Lambeth Palace Rd, London SE1 7LB. Telephone: 020 7401 8865. Website: www.gardenmuseum.org.uk

Gravetye Manor, Vowels Lane, West Hoathly, Sussex RH19 4LJ. (Managed as a hotel, with pre-booked tours of the garden available for small groups.) Telephone: 01342 810567. Website: www.gravetyemanor.co.uk

Levens Hall, Kendal, Cumbria LA8 0PD. Telephone: 01539 560321. Website: www.levenshall.co.uk

Osborne House, The Avenue, East Cowes, Isle of Wight PO32 6JX. Telephone: 01983 200022. Website: www.english-heritage.org.uk

Red House, Red House Lane, Bexleyheath, Kent DA6 8JF. Telephone: 020 8304 9878. Website: www.nationaltrust.org.uk

Regent's Park, The Store Yard, Inner Circle, Regent's Park, London NW1 4NR. Telephone: 0300 061 2300. Website: www.royalparks.gov.uk/The-Regents-Park

Royal Botanic Garden, Kew, Richmond, Surrey TW9 3AB. Telephone: 020 8332 5000. Website: www.kew.org

Standen, West Hoathly Road, East Grinstead, West Sussex RH19 4NE. Telephone: 01342 323029. Website: www.nationaltrust.org.uk

Trentham Gardens, Stone Road, Trentham, Stoke-on-Trent, Staffordshire ST4 8AX. Telephone: 01782 646646. Website: www.trentham.co.uk

Waddesdon Manor, Waddesdon, near Aylesbury, Buckinghamshire HP18 0JH. Telephone: 01296 653226. Website: www.nationaltrust.org.uk

FURTHER READING

Bisgrove, Richard. *William Robinson: The Wild Gardener*, Frances Lincoln, 2008

Conway, Hazel. *Public Parks*. Shire, 1996

Elliott, Brent. *Victorian Gardens*. Batsford, 1986

Hadfield, Miles. *A History of British Gardening*. Penguin, 1960

Hadfield, Miles. *Pioneers in Gardening*. Bloomsbury, 1996

Hitchmough, Wendy. *Arts and Crafts Gardens*. Pavilion, 1997

Hobhouse, Penelope. *Plants in Garden History*. Pavilion, 1992

Jekyll, Gertrude. *Colour in the Flower Garden*. Reed International, 1995

Musgrave, Toby et al. *The Plant Hunters*. Ward Lock, 1998

Quest-Ritson, Charles. *The English Garden: A Social History*. Viking, 2001

Robinson, William. *The Wild Garden*. Timber Press, 1994

Way, Twigs. *Topiary*. Shire, 2010

INDEX

Page numbers in italics refer to illustrations